FR. JOHN BOSCO ODONGO,CM., SSL

The Role
of the
Mother of Jesus
in the
Gospel of John

An Exegetical Study of
John 2, 1-12; 19, 25-27

Paperback: 978-1-968667-39-9
Hardcover: 978-1-968667-46-7
eBook: 978-1-968667-40-5
Library of Congress Control Number: 2025916013

This is a work of nonfiction.

Ordering Information:

Prime Seven Media
518 Landmann St.
Tomah City, WI 54660

Printed in the United States of America

DEDICATION

I dedicate this work to the Very Rev. Fr. Tomaž Mavrič, CM., the superior general of the Congregation of the Mission and to all my confreres worldwide. Also, to the visitors of the Congregation of the mission western province of the United States of America and of the vice province of Kenya. I dedicate it also to my late father George Leandro Abok, my mum Rose Acio Obuga, my sisters Josephine Abok and family, Christine Nyana and family, Milly Apio and family, and brothers Geoffrey Ocaya and family, Dr. Justine Mike Okot and family, my aunty Jacinta Acen and the entire family, Awila clan, Owaka clan, Marlene Maria and family, Karl in Malta, Inge, Rolf, Linda Rainer Matzewitski and Linda, late Waltraut Peter, Bea Hanne, and their entire families, Sr. Arthur Gordon, D.C., Sr. Deborah, D.C., Sr. Caridad, D.C., late Sr. Bernadette, Steve Kelly and family, Vickie Black and family, Barbara O Thibodeau and family, Rich Bell and family, Constansia Alela and family, Rose Ewin and family, Late Francis Ogwal Ave Maria, Rita, Maria, Celestino, Anna and family, Amedeo, Vania, Stefano, Matteo, Giulia, Anna, Cinzia and their families, Franca, Giuseppe, Patrizia, Silvana, Antonina, Alessandro, Martina, Angelo, Maria Grazia Tantillo, Carlo, Lia, Angelo, Chiara, Beatrice Sande Abuni and the entire family of the Association Bambino Uganda.

The work is also dedicated to His lordship the Rt. Rev. Claudio Cipolla, bishop of the diocese of Padua in Italy and to the entire diocese of Padua , his Lordship the Rt. Rev. Sanctus Wanok, bishop of Lira catholic diocese in Uganda, Msgr. Luigi Beggiao Superior of the house of the clergy at Padua and the entire community of the "Casa del Clero padua", Lorenzo Don Biasion parish priest of San Giorgio delle Pertiche and the entire Christian community, Lucia Petrin, Paolo Pierluigi, Matteo, Alessio, and Davide, Grande Roberta, De Stefano Salva, Romani Alberto, Drogheria Bruna, Romani Davide, Romani Valentina, Milde Magnani, Claudia Costa, Paola, Luigia, Francesco, Luna, Diamante, Tonino, late Sabino and Patrizia and their family, Rita and family, Michela Bovo, Basso Alberto, Giulia, Andrea, Sara, Zoccarato Giuseppe and Toto Paola, Tombolato Afra, Simeonato Enrico, Marina Anselmi, Monica Scapin and Bruno and family, Sr. Carol Raffaela Prevedello of the Crucified Christ, Sr. Anna Maria, Sr. Tiziana, Sr. Leo, Grande Brunilde, Ciro D'Onofrio, Marzia Chieragatti, Tiziana Chieragatti, Grande Simona, Annamaria Covelli, Fernanda Covelli, Marina Corona, Benedetto, Maria, Lucia, Luciana, Carla, Giuseppe, Nadia, Rosetta, Gian Luca, Ilenia, Elisa, Gloria, Christine Buggio, Vittorino Rigatti and family, Jessica Afwande and Dismas Afwande and the entire family. I continue to dedicate this work to: Minuzzi Lina, Pivotto Graziano, Allegro Giuseppe, Pilotto Teresa, Allegro Giovanni, Phan Tran Yen Thi-Celine, Liviana, Vellia, Loredana, Maddalena, Carla, Rev. Dr. Gary Müller, CM Rev. Rich Wehrmeyer, CM Rev. Fr. Thomas Nyambunde, CM.,JCL, Liviana Gonzales. Great thanks to all for standing with me. Thanks to all the benefactors, friends and indeed everyone who has helped me to accomplish this task by their prayers, affection, moral, spiritual, intellectual and material support. May God bless you all abundantly.

Review: Reviewed by Cherubimaris Casino for Readers' Favorite

The Role of the Mother of Jesus in the Gospel of John by Fr. John Bosco Odongo is based on his thesis for the Pontifical Biblical Institute in Rome, which explores the role of Jesus' mother. It references two key events from John's Gospel: the Wedding at Cana (John 2:1-12) and the Crucifixion (John 19:25-27). The work is a deep but approachable look at Mary, the mother of Jesus. The study provides scriptural foundations for anyone curious about her theological significance. The work is divided into three parts. The first part focuses on the Wedding at Cana, where Mary notices the shortage of wine and asks Jesus to intervene. The second part focuses on Mary at the foot of the cross. She stands by Jesus in his darkest hour as he entrusts Mary to his beloved disciple, John. This establishes her as a mother figure for the Church and a companion in Jesus' suffering. The final chapter ties it all together, painting Mary as an intercessor, a maternal presence, a quiet listener, who leads others to her son. The author culminates his study with a personal reflection on having devotion to Mary and how it has impacted his work as a Vincentian priest and missionary. I found the writing to be highly academic, employing narrative criticism with Greek etymology, supported by a bibliography of scholarly works. Fr. John Bosco Odongo engages with key commentators like Brown, Keener, and Zumstein, offering a balanced discussion of Mary's symbolic roles, such as the "new Eve" or representative of Israel, while acknowledging discussions about her as a co-redemptrix. The personal reflections in the final chapter are accessible and inspiring. As a Catholic educator, I highly recommend The Role of the Mother of Jesus in the Gospel of John for those seeking to enrich their biblical knowledge and Marian devotion. It is a great read for scholars, the clergy, and those interested in Mary, encouraging deeper reflection on faith, obedience, and accompaniment.

Review: Reviewed by Danelle Petersen for Readers' Favorite

Divided into three parts, The Role of the Mother of Jesus in the Gospel of John by Father John Bosco is a thesis topic on Jesus' mother, Mary, and the pivotal role she plays in the church. Different theories are explored concerning her motives, and a beautiful picture is painted. Her character suggests that she was a woman of strength, resilience, and a problem solver, as she first noticed the lack of wine at the wedding celebration in Cana. She was also a good listener and obedient follower of Jesus Christ, a vital characteristic as a person of faith. In this book, Mary's choices are discussed by fellow theologians who offer special insight into who Mary was and why she deserves her place next to the Son. Father John discusses Mary's life choices and quotes passages from the Bible, providing proof as to why Mary's influence is so substantial. In his most vulnerable state, Jesus appointed Mary as the Mother Divine, a title she still holds today. Reading The Role of the Mother Jesus in the Gospel of John was a wonderful experience, as I have never looked beyond Mary as anything other than the Messiah's mother. I was pleasantly surprised to learn she plays an equally important role in the faith. Reading the passages of John with fresh eyes, I recognized the Mary whom Father John so deftly describes. Mary was not merely a vessel used to carry the Messiah. She was chosen for her leadership skills, observance, and compassionate nature. Father John Bosco's easy writing style and warm tone contributed to the pleasure I experienced while reading. I encourage fellow followers of Christ to explore Father John's works and the important role Mary plays in the faith. The bibliography section also offers interesting studies for further reading.

Review: Reviewed by Joe Wisinski for Readers' Favorite

To many Christians, Mary, the mother of Jesus, is an important part of their faith. Fr. John Bosco Odongo wrote The Role of the Mother of Jesus in the Gospel of John to teach readers about Jesus and Mary's relationship. The study is limited to specific passages of the Bible. The first chapter focuses on John 2, verses 1-12, which is the story of the wedding in Cana of Galilee. The second chapter, which studies John 19:25-27, is about Jesus' mother at the foot of the cross. The final chapter is a summary chapter, looking over the entire role of the mother of Jesus, with an emphasis on the theological implications. Odongo used the original Greek as the basis for his work, but translated the Greek words into English. The book contains detailed footnotes, including references to many other works, and ends with an extensive bibliography. The Role of the Mother of Jesus in the Gospel of John is a fascinating book. Fr. John Bosco Odongo did wide-ranging research, and it shows in his meticulous treatment of this topic. Although it's an exegetical, scholarly work, anyone with an interest in the topic will find this to be both a useful and inspiring book. It would be especially beneficial for those in theological studies, whether they're in college or grad school. I liked that Odongo's book looked at more than one possible interpretation of the passages, as a work of this nature should. The same goes for how the author dealt judiciously with the issue surrounding the difficulty of correct interpretation. Odongo's portrayal of the relationship between Jesus and Mary is positive, which accurately reflects the biblical passages that he discusses. I heartedly recommend this fine work.

EPIGRAPH

[5]λέγει ἡ μήτηρ αὐτοῦ τοῖς διακόνοις Ὅ τι ἂν λέγῃ ὑμῖν, ποιήσατε (His mother said to the servants, "Do whatever he tells you" (John 2,5, RSV Second Catholic Edition). [26]Ἰησοῦς οὖν ἰδὼν τὴν μητέρα καὶ τὸν μαθητὴν παρεστῶτα ὃν ἠγάπα, λέγει τῇ μητρί Γύναι, ἴδε ὁ υἱός σου. [27] εἶτα λέγει τῷ μαθητῇ Ἴδε ἡ μήτηρ σου. καὶ ἀπ' ἐκείνης τῆς ὥρας ἔλαβεν ὁ μαθητὴς αὐτὴν εἰς τὰ ἴδια (When Jesus saw his mother, and the disciple whom he loved standing near, he said to his mother, "Woman, behold, your son!" [27] Then he said to the disciple, "Behold, your mother!" And from that hour the disciple took her to his own home (John 19, 26 - 27, RSV Second Catholic Edition).

Acknowledgments

I sincerely acknowledge the great, generous, kind and gracious support from Rev. Prof. Kamanzi Michel Segatara, S.J., professors and fellow colleagues biblists at the Pontifical Biblical institute in Rome, Italy. I extend my acknowledgement to Very Rev. Fr. Edwin Mugwe, CM., previous visitor and Very Rev. Benson Odhiambo, CM., the current Visitor of the Vice Province of Kenya, very Rev. Patrick J. McDevitt, C.M., previous visitor of the Congregation of the Mission Western Province of the United States of America, Very Rev. Dr. Fr. Thomas Esselman, CM., assistant provincial superior of the Congregation of the Mission western Province of the United states of America, and finally to the very Rev. Fr. Joe Williams, CM., the current visitor of the Congregation of the Mission Western province and all the confreres of the same province for their generous sacrifices towards my priestly and biblical formation. I acknowledge the generous and kind support of the house superior of "Collegio Apostolic Leoniano Roma" Fr. Giancarlo Passerini, CM., Very Rev. Fr. Valerio Francesco di Trapani, CM., visitor and the entire Congregation of the Mission province of Italy and finally the students and the community of Collegio Apostolico Leoniano.

ABBREVIATIONS

CBQ	Catholic Biblical Quarterly
DNTB	Dictionary of New Testament Background
Exod	Exodus
Gen	Genesis
GNC	Good News Commentaries
Isa	Isaiah
Jer	Jeremiah
JTS	The Journal of Theological Studies
Lev	Leviticus
Macc	Maccabees
Matt	Matthew
NTL	The New Testament Library
Rev	Revelation
Sam	Samuel
SE	Studia Evangelica
Sir	Sirach
WBC	Word Biblical Commentary

TABLE OF CONTENTS

GENERAL INTRODUCTION

1. Topic

This book will discuss "the role of the mother of Jesus in the Gospel of John: An Exegetical Study of John 2,1-12; John 19, 25-27".

2. Aim of the book

This book aims to discover the role of the mother of Jesus and its theological implications in John 2, 1-12 and John 19, 25-27. This discovery will be done by answering the following questions: (a) What is the role of the mother of Jesus in John 2, 1-12 and John 19, 25-27? (b) Why is the name of the mother of Jesus not used in John 2, 1-12 and John 19, 25-27? (c) Point out the theological implications of the role of the mother of Jesus in John 2,1-12 and John 19, 25-27.

3. Methodology

This book will proceed using a narrative criticism and a close reading of John 2, 1-12; John 19, 25-27. Since these texts are related to other texts in the Old and New Testaments, the book will consider studying them from the intratextual and intertextual perspectives as well.

4. Itinerary of the study

This book will have three chapters in total. The first chapter will be based on the exegetical study of John 2,1-12 and the second chapter will be dedicated to the exegesis of John 19, 25-27. The third chapter will be concerned with the theological implications of the exegetical study of the role of the mother of Jesus in John 2,1-12; 19, 25-27. Let us see what each chapter will contain.

The first chapter will focus on the mother of Jesus at the wedding at Cana of Galilee (John 2, 1-12). It shall be introduced and proceed with preliminary matters: context of John 2, 1-12 (the immediate context of John 2, 1-12; the global context of John 2, 1-12), delimitation of John 2, 1-12, Textual Criticism of John 2, 1-12, text and translation of John 2,1-12, Narrative Structure of John 2,1-12 according to Matand, brief explanation of the concentric structure of Matand, narrative analysis of John 2, 1-12: initial situation presented in John 2, 1-2 (Καὶ τῇ ʽἡμέρᾳ τῇ τρίτῃ , "and on the third day" in John 2,1; γάμος ἐγένετο, "a wedding took place" in John 2,1; ἐν Κανὰ τῆς Γαλιλαίας, "in Cana of Galilee" in John 2,1), main characters will be introduced in John 2, 1-2: ἡ μήτηρ τοῦ Ἰησοῦ, "the mother of Jesus" (2,1); οἱ μαθηταὶ αὐτοῦ, "his disciples" (John 2, 2). This chapter will also contain items such as the mother of Jesus acted to solve the problem (John 2, 3-5): οἶνον οὐκ ἔχουσιν, "they have not wine" (John 2, 3); τί ἐμοὶ καὶ σοί, γύναι; "what to me and to you, woman?" (John 2, 4); ἡ ὥρα , "the hour" (John 2, 4); ὅ τι ἂν λέγῃ ὑμῖν ποιήσατε, "do whatever he tells you" (John 2, 5); the mother of Jesus turned τοῖς διακόνοις "to the servants"(John 2, 5) and the importance of the instruction of the Mother of Jesus in John 2, 5. It will move on to discuss transformative action (John 2, 6-8), the reaction of the steward (John 2, 9-10), and final situation (John 2, 11-12). It will also look at key elements in John 2, 1-12. In doing so we shall discuss the term "Sign" in John 2, 11 (the purpose of the sign: revelation of his glory as in John 2, 11; the usefulness of the glory of Jesus revealed in John 2, 11), setting of John 2,1-12 by considering the place to be Cana of Galilee as presented in John 2, 1; the third day as in John 2, 1; and the wedding custom in John 2, 2-3a. Since our text is related to some other texts in both the Old and New testaments, we shall also look at their intratextual and intertextual links. Then finally we shall look at the mother of Jesus at the wedding at Cana of Galilee (John 2, 1-12) and conclude.

The second chapter will be dedicated to the exegesis of John 19, 25-27 with a focus on the mother of Jesus at the foot of the cross (John 19, 25-27). This chapter will be introduced then followed by the preliminary matters including context of John 19, 25-27, delimitation of John 19, 25-27, an issue of exegetical interpretation in John 19, 25 (two women, three women, four women), text and translation of John 19, 25-27, narrative structure and analysis :plot of John 19, 25-27 (Initial situation in John 19, 25; Complication (John 19, 26a); Transformative action (John 19, 26b-27a); and finally we look at the resolution and final situation in John 19, 27b. This chapter will also discuss key elements in John 19, 25-27 by looking at the women by the cross (John 19, 25); γύναι, "woman" (John 19, 26a); and ἀπ' ἐκείνης τῆς ὥρας "from that hour" (John 19, 27). It will continue studying Setting of John 19, 25 – 27, intratextual and Intertextual connections with other texts within the Old and New Testaments, the mother of Jesus and the beloved disciple at the foot of the Cross and will conclude.

The third chapter will be the last chapter of this book. In it we will discuss the theological implications of the exegetical study of the Role of the Mother of Jesus in John 2, 1-12; 19, 25-27. The chapter will be introduced and embark on discussing the role of the mother of Jesus in John 2, 1-12; 19, 25-27. We shall do this by looking at the mother of Jesus as a mother who believed in her son, a problem solver and friend, initiator, organizer, and collaborator, the commander and a good instructor (John 2,5),a silent listener, a companion of Jesus in good and bad times, a mother of the beloved disciple and the brethren. As a way of giving in more of my personal contribution, I will discuss what I learned as a reader from this exegetical study of John 2,1-12;19, 25-27 and the conclusion will be drawn.

This book will conclude with a general conclusion and bibliography will be presented.

5. Status *Quaestionis* (John 2,1-12 and John 19, 25-27)

Keener notes that the mother of Jesus functions as a role model of faith.[1] These two texts portray the mother of Jesus as one who is really a good companion to her son. She accompanied him both in good times, such as at the feast at Cana of Galilee (John 2, 1-12), where she participated vibrantly in the life and ministry of her son and also in bad times of the life of her son at the foot of the cross (John 19, 25-27). When viewed from the perspective of the title "woman," which Jesus uses to call his mother, she becomes a symbolic figure. In this regard, her role is as well symbolic in nature.[2] She represents Israel.[3] She is considered the "new Eve," hence "the mother of the new Israel."[4] She plays the role of being the mother

---

[1] Cf. C. S. KEENER., *Gospel of John*. A Commentary Vol 1 (Grand Rapids, MI, 2010) 509.

[2] Cf. R. E. BROWN., *Gospel According to John*. 2 Vols. (AB 29, 29A Garden City, N.Y, 1966-1970) 1:99.

[3] Cf. K. Hanhart., "The Structure of John i 35-iv 54", *Studies in John Presented to Professor Dr. J. N. Sevenster on the Occasion of His Seventieth Birthday* (ed. W. C. van Unnik) (NovTSup 24; Leiden, 1970) 41.

[4] E. C. Hoskyns., "Genesis I-III and St. John's Gospel", 21/83(Oxford April 1919) 211-212.

of the Church.[5] She is the model of faith (2, 3b-5) and instructor to the servants (John 2, 5).

Carson maintains that the mother of Jesus may play the role of "a representative of the church as a model of disciple, but only in the same way that other disciples in the narrative do...if we are tempted to view the mother's intercession as prefiguring a later role as mediatrix..."[6]

According to Zumstein, the mother of Jesus plays a great role in developing the plot from the "first scene" and later when her son performs the final act of revelation. She is a "textual signal" marking both the moments of starting and ending of the public ministry of her son Jesus.[7]

Moloney maintains that the mother of Jesus is the mother of the new family that Jesus created on the cross at the time of his death. He stated that this "passage" of John 19,25-27 "affirms the maternal role of the mother of Jesus in this new family of Jesus."[8]

---

[5] A. Feuillet., *Johannine Studies* (trans. E. C. Thomas) (Staten Island, N. Y 1964) 35; T. L. Broodie., *The Gospel according to John*. A Literary and Theological Commentary (New York 1993) 174-175; R. A. Culpepper., *Anatomy of the Fourth Gospel*. A Study in Literary Design (Philadelphia 1983) 134. According to Manelli, the mother of Jesus plays a role of "madre di Cristo e madre degli uomini" in Italian language meaning, "the mother of Christ and of men/human beings". He adds that she is the mother of the members of Christ. That this new motherhood of Mary generated by faith is the fruit of new love, which will mature at the foot of the cross through her participation in the redemptive love of her son Jesus. She plays the role of both spiritual and universal motherhood at the foot of the cross. See S. M. Manelli., *Mariologia Biblica* (Frigento, AV 2005) 400. Many catholic exegetes affirm A. Feuillet, accepting to see in John 19, 25-27 at least an insinuation of the spiritual motherhood of Mary. See A. Feuillet., *Maria*. Madre del Messia, Madre della Chiesa (Milano, 2004) 42. Mary is the divine mother at the foot of the cross according to Manelli. Cf. S. M. Manelli., *Mariologia Biblica*, 401.

[6] Cf. D. A. CARSON., *The Gospel according to John* (Grand Rapids 1991) 168.

[7] Cf. J. Zumstein., "The Mother of Jesus and the Beloved Disciple: How a New Family is Established under the Cross" in Characters Studies in the Fourth Gospel (S. A. Hunt., — D.F. Tolmie., — R. Zimmermann., eds.,) (Tübingen 2013) 644.

[8] F. J. Moloney., "John", *Paulist Biblical Commentary* (eds. J. E. A. Chiu., et al.) (New York—Mahwah, NJ 2018) 1173.

Some scholars like Allegra and Laconi holds the view that the mother of Jesus plays the role of co-redemptrix in the gospel of John; that is, she joins her son, the crucified redeemer, in bringing about redemption. The divine mother is present at the cross. She gets intimately united with her dying son, Jesus, on the cross as our co-redemptrix.[9]

Brown and other scholars hold the view that Mary stands out as one who believed in Jesus as a "wonder-worker." This is the belief that she demonstrates in John 2, 3. She plays the role of a mother to the beloved disciple and a model of belief and discipleship.[10]

6. The Scope and Limitation of the Study

This work will try to make a humble contribution to the role of the mother of Jesus in John 2,1-12 and John 19, 25-27. The theological implications of the role of the mother of Jesus in John 2,1-12 and John 19,25-27 may encourage Marian devotions in our world today. This book will not claim to exhaust everything concerning the role of the mother of Jesus in John 2,1-12 and John 19,25-27. This book endeavors to arouse new insights in the readers to do more research.

---

[9]   Cf. G. M. Allegra., *Il Cuore Immacolato di Maria* (Acireale 1991)132. In this same line of thought, Laconi adds that the mission of Mary, even though wrapped up in the supernatural, is characterized by one constant element called pain which consecrated her the co-redeemer next to the suffering Jesus. Cf. M. Laconi., "Theotokos", *Maria nel Nuovo Testamento, Enciclopedia Mariana* (Genova— Milano, 1959) 37.

[10] Cf. R. E. Brown., et al (eds)., *Mary in the New Testament.* A Collaborative Assessment by Protestant and Roman Catholic Scholars (New York— Mahwah 1978) 287.

CHAPTER I

The mother of Jesus at the wedding at Cana of Galilee (John 2, 1-12)

1.0 Introduction

This first chapter focuses on the mother of Jesus at the wedding of Cana of Galilee (John 2, 1-12). John begins his presentation of the public ministry of Jesus with a narrative of the pericope concerned with the first sign of Jesus. This episode reveals the glory of Jesus and the role of the mother of Jesus as an intercessor and model of trusting faith in Jesus. It further reveals to us that the mother of Jesus is a commander (John 2, 5), an organizer as she talked with her son and the servants, organizing them for a common activity and goal. She is a problem solver as she noticed the problem at hand and went forward, initiating a process of getting the solution to it. She is a good and conscious companion to the son in times of celebrations (as she kept alert to what was going on in her environment and discovered the challenge of the lack of wine in the home where the wedding was taking place), a woman who never takes offense.[11] This text led the disciples to believe in Jesus (John 2, 11). It also invites the reader

---

[11] For example, in John 2,4 Jesus called his mother "woman" and she never bothered about it.

to believe in Jesus. This pericope also highlights the last words of the mother of Jesus and the importance of obedience to the word of Jesus.

This chapter shall proceed with preliminary matters: context of John 2, 1-12 (the immediate context of John 2, 1-12; the global context of John 2, 1-12), delimitation of John 2, 1-12, textual criticism of John 2, 1-12, and text and translation of John 2,1-12. We shall move on to study the narrative structure of John 2,1-12 according to Matand and give a brief explanation of the concentric structure of Matand. We shall also do a narrative analysis of John 2, 1-12: initial situation presented in John 2, 1-2 (Καὶ τῇ ἡμέρᾳ τῇ τρίτῃ , "and on the third day" in John 2,1; γάμος ἐγένετο, "a wedding took place" in John 2,1; ἐν Κανὰ τῆς Γαλιλαίας, "in Cana of Galilee" in John 2,1), main characters will be introduced in John 2, 1-2: ἡ μήτηρ τοῦ Ἰησοῦ, "the mother of Jesus" (2,1); οἱ μαθηταὶ αὐτοῦ, "his disciples" (John 2, 2). This chapter will move on to look at other themes like : the mother of Jesus acted to solve the problem in John 2, 3-5 : οἶνον οὐκ ἔχουσιν, "they have not wine" (John 2, 3); τί ἐμοὶ καὶ σοί, γύναι; "what to me and to you, woman?" (John 2, 4); ἡ ὥρα, "the hour" (John 2, 4); ὅ τι ἂν λέγῃ ὑμῖν ποιήσατε, "do whatever he tells you" (John 2, 5); the mother of Jesus turned τοῖς διακόνοις "to the servants"(John 2, 5) and the importance of the instruction of the Mother of Jesus in John 2, 5. It will discuss also transformative action (John 2, 6-8), the reaction of the steward (John 2, 9-10), and final situation (John 2, 11-12). The chapter will continue discussing the key elements in John 2, 1-12 by studying and presenting the term "Sign" in John 2, 11 (the purpose of the sign: revelation of his glory as in John 2, 11; the usefulness of the glory of Jesus revealed in John 2, 11), setting of John 2,1-12 by considering the place to be Cana of Galilee as presented in John 2, 1; the third day as in John 2, 1; and the wedding custom in John 2, 2-3a. Since our text is related to some other texts in both the Old and New testaments, we shall also look at their intratextual and intertextual links. Then finally we shall look at the mother of Jesus at the wedding at Cana of Galilee (John 2, 1-12) and conclude.

1.1 Preliminary Matters

This section will deal with Context of John 2,1-12, delimitation of the text, textual criticism, text and translation, and narrative structure.

1.1.1 Context of John 2, 1-12

This section will discuss this pericope's immediate and global context.

1.1.1.1 The immediate context of John 2, 1-12

This text is located in the Cana-to-Cana Cycle, which runs from John 2, 1 to 4, 54. [12] Our central focus is on the first part of this cycle (2, 1-12).

1.1.1.2 The global context of John 2, 1-12

This text is found in the book of the Signs, which runs from 1, 19 –12,50. This is the public ministry of Jesus. Through his words and signs, he revealed himself to his own people. He revealed himself as the revelation of his Father, but they rejected him. [13]

1.1.2 Delimitation of John 2, 1-12

John 2, 1-12 reveals the glory of Jesus and the first sign he performed at the wedding of Cana of Galilee. John 1, 19 - 51 is placed prior to this pericope, focusing on John the Baptist and his first disciples. It starts with v. 19 stating, "Καὶ αὕτη ἐστὶν ἡ μαρτυρία τοῦ Ἰωάννου, "and this is

---

[12] The Cana Cycle includes: the sign of marriage in Cana (John 2, 1-12), the new temple, not in Jerusalem (John 2, 13-22), salvation for which God gave his only son (John 3,1-21), judgment for which God gave his son everything (John 3, 22-36), new temple: not in Gerizim (John 4,1-42) and healing miracle in Cana (John 4, 43-54).

[13] See R. E. Brown., *The Gospel According to John I-XII*. A New Translation with Introduction and Commentary (AYB 29; New Haven— London 2008) CXXXVIII.

the testimony of John" and ends with v. 51 "καὶ λέγει αὐτῷ· ἀμὴν ἀμὴν λέγω ὑμῖν, ὄψεσθε τὸν οὐρανὸν ἀνεῳγότα καὶ τοὺς ἀγγέλους τοῦ θεοῦ ἀναβαίνοντας καὶ καταβαίνοντας ἐπὶ τὸν υἱὸν τοῦ ἀνθρώπου," "amen, amen, I say to you, you will see the heavens opened, and the angels of God ascending and descending upon the son of man."

Then John 2, 1-12 begins with v.1 "Καὶ τῇ ἡμέρᾳ τῇ τρίτῃ γάμος ἐγένετο ἐν Κανὰ τῆς Γαλιλαίας, καὶ ἦν ἡ μήτηρ τοῦ Ἰησοῦ ἐκεῖ·", "and on the third day, there was a marriage at Cana in Galilee, and the mother of Jesus was there" and ends with 2, 12 Μετὰ τοῦτο κατέβη εἰς Καφαρναοὺμ αὐτὸς καὶ ἡ μήτηρ αὐτοῦ καὶ οἱ ἀδελφοὶ [αὐτοῦ] καὶ οἱ μαθηταὶ αὐτοῦ καὶ ἐκεῖ ἔμειναν οὐ πολλὰς ἡμέρας, "after this, he went down to Capernaum, with his mother and his brethren and his disciples; and there they stayed for a few days".[14] John 2, 13 is the beginning of a new textual unit saying Καὶ ἐγγὺς ἦν τὸ πάσχα τῶν Ἰουδαίων, καὶ ἀνέβη εἰς Ἱεροσόλυμα ὁ Ἰησοῦς, "and the Passover of the Jews was drawing near, and Jesus went up to Jerusalem."

1.1.3 Textual Criticism of John 2, 1-12

The usage of ὑστερήσαντος οἴνου, "the wine gave out" (John 2, 3). Brown maintains that some commentators have made a preference for the longer reading of the Sinaiticus and of the OL: οινον ουκ ειχον οτι συνετελεσθη ο οινος του γαμου ειτα, "they have no wine, for the wine provided for the feast had been used up." However, the lectio brevior is

---

[14] A number of scholars maintain that this pericope starts with v.1 and ends with v.11 because ἐν Κανὰ τῆς Γαλιλαίας, "In Cana of Galilee" found in v.1 and v.11 forms an inclusio. The presence of Μετὰ τοῦτο κατέβη εἰς Καφαρναοὺμ , "after this he went down to Capernaum" in v. 12 indicates to us that the place is no longer Cana of Galilee but Capernaum. This means there is a change of place and of episode. Therefore, v.11 ends the pericope, and a new unit begins with v.12. I prefer taking it as it begins from v.1 and ends in v.12 for the reasons explained already in the text.

supported by Bodmer Papyri.[15] Barrett maintains that the use of ὑστερεῖν in the sense provided in this verse, "the wine had run out," is late, and a copyist may have wished to convey a vivid message that no wine at all was left.[16] Beasley-Murray thinks that just after the conclusion of the 'statement' there are "some OL mss and syr^hmg add: ὅτι συνετελέσθη ὁ οἶνος τοῦ ἁμου· εἶτα, "since the wine for the wedding was used up; then...."[17]

Metzger maintains that ὑστερήσαντος οἴνου has been paraphrased by 'reading' οἶνον οὐκ εἶχον, ὅτι συνετελέσθη ὁ οἶνος τοῦ γάμου· εἶτα, "They had no wine because the wine of the wedding feast had been used up; then ...". He adds that "two Old Latin witnesses (it^e,) describe the situation as...et factum est per multam turbam vocitorum vinum consummari, "It happened that because of the great crowd of those who had been invited, the wine was finished. The 'shorter reading, adopted'... is attested by 𝔓^66, ℵ and all known uncial and minuscule manuscripts, as well as all versional witnesses not cited above".[18]

About the hour, Beasley-Murray states that it is tenable from a grammatical perspective to consider οὔπω ἥκει ἡ ὥρα μου like a question. The question would be, 'has not my hour now arrived?' This "hour" being referred to can relate to the messianic task of Jesus. This would delete the obstacle that Jesus did respond to the request of his mother despite 'an apparent rebuff.' The 'early Fathers' and a number of current exegetes from the Roman Catholic Church within the recent times prefer it. However, it is better to make a preference for the 'principle of difficilior lectio potior'[19] John 2, 12 used καὶ ἡ μήτηρ αὐτοῦ καὶ οἱ ἀδελφοὶ [αὐτοῦ] καὶ οἱ μαθηταὶ αὐτοῦ, "and his mother and his brothers and his disciples."

---

[15] See Brown., *The Gospel*, 98.

[16] See Barrett., *The Gospel According to St. John*, 190.

[17] G. R. Beasley-Murray., *John* (Word Biblical Commentary 36) (Waco, TX ²1999) 32.

[18] B. M. Metzger., *A Textual commentary on the Greek New Testament* (London — New York 1994) 172–173.

[19] Cf. G. R. BEASLEY-MURRAY., *John*, 32.

There are differences in the order of words and the 'omission of one' or extra words displayed in the manuscripts. For instance, αὐτοῦ which follows ἀδελφοί "is lacking in 𝔓⁶⁶*, B Ψ 0162 while αὐτοῦ, which follows μαθηταί, is not present in L 0141; then καὶ οἱ μαθηταὶ αὐτοῦ comes before καὶ ἡ μητήρ in Wˢᵘᵖᵖ... καὶ οἱ μαθηταὶ αὐτοῦ is lacking in ℵ al... due to the 'weight of the witnesses that lack the first αὐτοῦ' it may be better to put it inside 'square brackets.[20]

Why were the disciples of Jesus omitted from the original text? This is an interesting question to determine whether Jesus' disciples were mentioned in the original narrative text. In the ℵ , W, other OL mss, together with the Armenian, there is the omission of καὶ οἱ μαθηταὶ αὐτοῦ, "and his disciples" (John 2, 2; 2, 12). This view encouraged and supported Lindars in his belief that the disciples of Jesus were not mentioned in the original narrative text. This meant that the issue was related while Jesus was at home. This should be considered part of the folk legends narrated in the apocryphal gospels (127,132). However, he thinks that these speculations were not necessary for John 2, 12.[21]

1.1.4 Text and Translation of John 2,1-12

1.1.4.1 Text : John 2,1-12

1 Καὶ τῇ ʿἡμέρᾳ τῇ τρίτῃ' γάμος ἐγένετο ἐν ᵀ Κανὰ τῆς Γαλιλαίας, καὶ ἦν ἡ μήτηρ τοῦ Ἰησοῦ ἐκεῖ· 2 ἐκλήθη δὲ °καὶ ὁ Ἰησοῦς καὶ οἱ μαθηταὶ αὐτοῦ εἰς τὸν γάμον. 3 καὶ ʿὑστερήσαντος οἴνου' λέγει ἡ μήτηρ τοῦ Ἰησοῦ πρὸς αὐτόν· ʿοἶνον οὐκ ἔχουσιν'. 4 °[καὶ] λέγει αὐτῇ ὁ Ἰησοῦς· τί ἐμοὶ καὶ σοί, γύναι; οὔπω ἥκει ἡ ὥρα μου. 5 λέγει ἡ μήτηρ αὐτοῦ τοῖς διακόνοις· ʿὅ τι ἂν' λέγῃ ὑμῖν ποιήσατε. 6 ἦσαν δὲ ἐκεῖ λίθιναι ὑδρίαι ἓξ κατὰ τὸν καθαρισμὸν τῶν Ἰουδαίων °κείμεναι, χωροῦσαι ἀνὰ μετρητὰς δύο ἢ τρεῖς.

---

[20] B. M. Metzger., *A Textual commentary on the Greek New Testament*, 173.
[21] Cf. G. R. Beasley-Murray., *John*, 33.

7 ᵀλέγει αὐτοῖς ὁ Ἰησοῦς· γεμίσατε τὰς ὑδρίας ὕδατος. καὶ ἐγέμισαν αὐτὰς ἕως ἄνω. 8 καὶ λέγει αὐτοῖς· ἀντλήσατε νῦν καὶ φέρετε τῷ ἀρχιτρικλίνῳ· οἱ δὲ ἤνεγκαν. 9 ὡς δὲ ἐγεύσατο ὁ ἀρχιτρίκλινος τὸ ὕδωρ οἶνον γεγενημένον καὶ οὐκ ᾔδει πόθεν ἐστίν, οἱ δὲ διάκονοι ᾔδεισαν οἱ ἠντληκότες τὸ ὕδωρ, φωνεῖ τὸν νυμφίον ὁ ἀρχιτρίκλινος 10 καὶ λέγει αὐτῷ· πᾶς ἄνθρωπος ˢπρῶτον τὸν καλὸν οἶνον² τίθησιν καὶ ὅταν μεθυσθῶσιν ᵀ τὸν ἐλάσσω· σὺ τετήρηκας τὸν καλὸν οἶνον ἕως ἄρτι. 11 Ταύτην ⸀ἐποίησεν ἀρχὴν⸍ τῶν σημείων ὁ Ἰησοῦς ἐν Κανὰ τῆς Γαλιλαίας καὶ ἐφανέρωσεν τὴν δόξαν αὐτοῦ, καὶ ἐπίστευσαν εἰς αὐτὸν οἱ μαθηταὶ αὐτοῦ. 12 Μετὰ τοῦτο κατέβη εἰς Καφαρναοὺμ αὐτὸς καὶ ἡ μήτηρ αὐτοῦ καὶ οἱ ἀδελφοὶ ⸂[αὐτοῦ] καὶ οἱ μαθηταὶ αὐτοῦ⸃ καὶ ἐκεῖ ⸀ἔμειναν οὐ πολλὰς ἡμέρας. 13 ⸀Καὶ ἐγγὺς⸍ ἦν τὸ πάσχα τῶν Ἰουδαίων, καὶ ἀνέβη ⸂εἰς Ἱεροσόλυμα ὁ Ἰησοῦς⸃.

1.1.4.2 Translation[22]

1   On the third day, there was a wedding in Cana of Galilee, and the mother of Jesus was there.

2   Jesus and his disciples had also been invited to the wedding.

3   When the wine gave out, the mother of Jesus said to him, "They have no wine."

4   And Jesus said to her, "Woman, what concern is that to you and to me? My hour has not yet come."

5   His mother said to the servants, "Do whatever he tells you."

6   Now standing there were six stone water jars for the Jewish rites of purification, each holding twenty or thirty gallons.

7   Jesus said to them, "Fill the jars with water." And they filled them up to the brim.

---

[22] This translation of John 2,1-12 is adopted from *The Holy Bible: New Revised Standard Version Catholic Edition* (Washington, DC, 1993). I decided to adopt this because it is quite literal and makes a lot of sense in terms of literal and meaningful translation of the text into English language.

8 He said to them, "Now draw some out, and take it to the chief steward." So, they took it.

9 When the steward tasted the water that had become wine and did not know where it came from (though the servants who had drawn the water knew), the steward called the bridegroom.

10 and said to him, "Everyone serves the good wine first, and then the inferior wine after the guests have become drunk. But you have kept the good wine until now."

11 Jesus did this, the first of his signs, in Cana of Galilee, and revealed his glory; and his disciples believed in him.

12 After this he went down to Capernaum with his mother, his brothers, and his disciples; and they remained there a few days.

1.1.5 Narrative Structure of John 2,1-12 according to Matand[23]

A - Initial Situation (John 2,1-2)

B -The mother of Jesus acted to solve the problem (John 2,3-5)

C-Transformative Action (John 2,6-8)

B[1] - The reaction of the steward (John 2, 9-10)

A[1] - Final situation (John 2,11-12)

1.1.5.1 Brief explanation of the concentric structure of Matand

A- Initial situation (John 2, 1-2) and A[1] - Final situation (John 2, 11-12) introduce and conclude with time, place, circumstances, and characters. In B, the mother of Jesus initiates and organizes the transformative action

---

[23] For details about the concentric structure proposed by Matand, See J. M. Matand., "Head-Waiter and Bridegroom of the Wedding at Cana: Structure and Meaning of John 2,1-12", *JSNT* 30/1 (2007) 57.

process leading to the performance of the sign by Jesus (John 2, 3-5). She noticed the problem and, in faith, began to search for the solution in her son Jesus. She never gives up, even after a seemingly challenging question from her son. She does not get discouraged but believes that her son will finally do something. She organized the servants to be ready to do what Jesus would ask them to do (John 2, 5). C - Transformative action (John 2, 6-8) brings to us a transformation done by Jesus as a response to the implied request by his mother to him. Subsequently, C is the climax of this narrative structure where Jesus speaks to the servants, and they obey. Jesus obeyed his mother in action by instructing the servants, who in turn obeyed him by doing what he asked them to do. His instruction was received by the servants his mother had already instructed in John 2, 5. This made the transformative action possible.

In these verses, we see Jesus and the servants' actions. Jesus responded to his mother's plea. He spoke to the servants, saying, "Fill the jars with water" (John 2, 7), and they obeyed by filling the jars up to the brim (John 2, 7). Jesus told them, "Now draw some out and take it to the steward of the feast."(John 2, 8). The text reports, "So they took it"(John 2, 8). Jesus's transformative actions and the servants' obedience and action lead to a sign (John 2, 6-8). In B¹, we see the reaction of the steward of the feast (John 2, 9-10). It is reported that as soon as he tasted the water that had become wine and did not know where it was from, he called upon the bridegroom. This steward said to the bridegroom πᾶς ἄνθρωπος πρῶτον τὸν καλὸν οἶνον τίθησιν καὶ ὅταν μεθυσθῶσιν τὸν ἐλάσσω· σὺ τετήρηκας τὸν καλὸν οἶνον ἕως ἄρτι, "Every man serves the good wine first; and when men have drunk freely, then the poor wine; but you have kept the good wine until now." (John 2, 10).

1.2 Narrative Analysis of John 2, 1-12

Here is an analysis of the different sub-units: Initial Situation (John 2, 1-2), the mother of Jesus initiates and organizes the transformative action process (John 2, 3-5), Jesus speaks, and the servants obey (2, 6-8), the headwaiter reacts(2, 9-10) and the final situation (John 2, 11-12).

1.2.1 Initial Situation (John 2, 1-2)

The first two verses introduce both the time this transformative action took place and the geographical locus. The initial situation also names the event and the characters in the action.

1.2.1.1 Καὶ τῇ ʽἡμέρᾳ τῇ τρίτῃ ("and on the third day") (John 2,1)

This textual sub-unit begins with Καὶ τῇ ἡμέρᾳ τῇ τρίτῃ ("and on the third day") (John 2,1). This statement describes time. It connects with the preceding and continues with the sequence of times already given in John 1, 29.35.43, which was meant to focus on the summoning of the disciples and pointing forward. According to Barret, the series of the events about the disciples ended in 2,11.[24]

It is problematic to get the real meaning of the above expression. The events began in John 1,19-28, followed by "the next day" (see John 1, 29-34; 1, 35-42;1, 43-51). However, John 2, 1-12 began with the "on the third day." In trying to explain this phrase, Theodore notes that it is the third day after the baptism by John (John 1, 29-34). So, the days would be arranged as follows: the first day (John 1, 35-42), the second day (John 1,43-51), and the third day falls on John 2, 1. According to Brown, most exegetes prefer to count from the day of the encounter of Philip and Nathaniel in John 1, 43-51. He maintains 'that day and the next day' were traveling days from Jordan to the valley of Galilee.[25]

Barrett argues that the Greek use of τῇ ʽἡμέρᾳ τῇ τρίτῃ ("on the third day") means "the day after tomorrow" which might have been counted

---

[24] See C. K. Barrett., *The Gospel according to John*, 189.

[25] See Brown., *The Gospel According to John*, 97.

from the day mentioned last. Six complete days could be counted, while the fifth day may be used for traveling. He is not sure about its certainty.[26] The "third day" might refer to the day following the previous days in the narrative sequence. Schnakenburg notes that the "third day" may carry with it a great significance if it symbolically refers to the resurrection of Jesus. This could hold water if the "hour" of Jesus referred to his glorification, and the first sign he did at Cana remains as anticipation and the promise of this authentic revelation.[27]

This "third day" could also refer to the theophany in Exod 19, 10-11.15-16, which relates to the week of preparation at Sinai. In this text, the Lord said to Moses, " Go to the people and consecrate them today and tomorrow, and let them wash their garments" (Exod 19, 10), "and be ready by the third day; for on the third day the Lord will come down upon Mount Sinai in the sight of all the people" (Exod 19,11), "be ready by the third day; do not go near a woman" (Exod 19, 15), and "on the morning of the third day there was thunder and lightning, and a thick cloud upon the mountain, and a very loud trumpet blast so that all the people who were in the camp trembled" (Exod 19,16). The third day in both could be a time of preparation for the event in question.

1.2.1.2 γάμος ἐγένετο, "a wedding took place" (2,1)

The expression γάμος ἐγένετο," a wedding took place"(v. 1), explains the event that took place and upon which Jesus performed the first sign. Zerwick and Grosvenor agree that the Greek word γάμος means "marriage or wedding ceremony."[28] According to Brown, culturally,

---

[26] See Barret., *The Gospel according to John*,190.

[27] See R. Schnackenburg., *The Gospel According to St. John*. Introduction and Commentary on Chapters 1-4 (trans. K. Smyth) (New York, 1982) I, 325.

[28] M. S. J. Zerwick.,— M. A. Grosvenor., *Grammatical Analysis of the Greek New Testament* (Rome 2016) 289.

around the first century, the Jews held weddings publicly in a procession. The bridegroom's friends would bring the bride to the groom's house. The wedding supper and feast lasted for about seven days.[29]

1.2.1.3 ἐν Κανὰ τῆς Γαλιλαίας, "in Cana of Galilee" (John 2,1)

The reference to Cana in Galilee is common in the gospel of John. He refers to it four times (Cf. John 2, 1.11; 4, 46; 21, 2) probably in accordance with the tradition (Cf. 4,46; 21,2). Barret holds the view that the genitive Κανὰ τῆς Γαλιλαίας, "Cana of Galilee"(v. 1), was meant to identify a particular Cana and also to show that the first sign did not happen in Judea but in Galilee.[30]

1.2.1.4 Main characters introduced (John 2, 1-2)

In these two verses, the main characters are introduced. They are Jesus, his mother, and his disciples.

1.2.1.4.1 ἡ μήτηρ τοῦ Ἰησοῦ, "the mother of Jesus" (2,1)

The mother of Jesus was not called by her specific name in the Gospel of John. This is attested in 2,1 ("the mother of Jesus"); 2,12 ("his mother"); 6,42 ("is not this Jesus, the son of Joseph, whose father and mother we know?); 19,25 (his mother...his mother's sister...) where her name is never mentioned. She is simply identified with her son Jesus. This may not be an omission. Referring to her as "mother of Jesus" is a mark of respect. Nevertheless, in the gospel of John, anonymity may mean a sign of intimacy rather than obscurity.[31] The fact that her name is not mentioned in the text is not a problem of necessity.

---

[29] See R. E. Brown., *The Gospel According to John,* 98.
[30] See C. K. Barret., *The Gospel according to John,*190.
[31] See J. A. Brant., *John* (PCNT; Grand Rapids, MI 2011) 56.

1.2.1.4.2 οἱ μαθηταὶ αὐτοῦ, "his disciples" (John 2, 2)

John 1, 35-51 describes the call of the first disciples namely Andrew (John 1,40), Simon (John 1,42), Philip (John 1,43), and Nathaniel (John 1, 45-49). We do not have any other vocation stories written, even though in 6,67, there is a mention of "the twelve." According to Barret, this entire group of disciples is referred to in this pericope by John the Evangelist.[32]

1.2.2 The mother of Jesus acted to solve the problem (John 2, 3-5)

1.2.2.1 οἶνον οὐκ ἔχουσιν, "they have not wine" (John 2, 3)

The text reveals that the ὑστερήσαντος οἴνου, "having been deficient of wine"(John 2, 3). At this point they lacked wine. Brown holds the view that the mother of Jesus learned of the lack of wine and initiated the process of getting the solution. The mother of Jesus was deeply concerned with this situation because a tradition held that she was the bridegroom's aunt, identified as John, son of Zebedee in the third-century Latin preface. Also, tradition maintains that Salome, mother of John and wife of Zebedee, was the sister of Mary. This means John is the cousin of Jesus.[33] Therefore, the mother of Jesus was right to initiate the process and organization of the transformative action, leading to the solution of the problem. This is why she went to her son Jesus and told him οἶνον οὐκ ἔχουσιν, "They have no wine"(John 2, 3). This meant that she was an observant and practical person. She is realistic. She goes out to act more practically to save the embarrassing situation, for It was disgraceful to run out of wine. Running out of wine in this kind of ceremony meant the loss of honor. It meant the groom and his family lacked the supply of wine

---

[32] See Barret., *The Gospel according to John*, 190.
[33] See Brown, *The Gospel According to John*, 98.

and the social connections and support to preserve the family's honor. Moreover, it also meant they lacked both social and material resources.[34]

Several commentators maintain that the mother of Jesus was requesting for a miracle. Schnackenburg notes that from the text, it is not clear that she was asking Jesus for a miracle but called the attention of Jesus to the lack of wine. He argues that this is ruled out by v. 5, in which the mother of Jesus is shown as a person who had faith in her son and, of course, a tranquil servant of Jesus, her son.[35] Nevertheless, Brown argues that the answer of Jesus in which he refuses to become involved may suggest that his mother demanded something from him.[36] Bennema argues on the contrary that "the statement of Jesus' mother is actually a request for Jesus to do something."[37] Derrett argues that the statement "they have no wine" in John 2, 3 ought to be read as an accusation against Jesus for having brought his disciples without enough gifts to take care of the expenses of the wedding ceremony. According to him, Jesus and his disciples are to be blamed to a certain extent for the wine which ran out.[38] This view of Derrett seems to be a bit weak because Jesus and his disciples were actually invited just like any other guests. This means the host family had planned for their guests, including Jesus and his disciples. Our text does not have evidence to support Derrett's idea about the accusation of Jesus and his disciples. If one goes that way, they may

---

[34] See R. H. Williams., "The Mother of Jesus at Cana. A Social- Science Interpretation of John 2, 1-12", *CBQ* 59 (1997) 684.

[35] See Schnackenburg., *The Gospel According to St. John,* 327. To this point of Schnackenburg, one would ask: Does having Faith preclude asking for a miracle? If anything, it is indeed Faith that pushes one to ask the Lord for something. So, his point seems to pose difficulty.

[36] See Brown., *The Gospel,* 98-99.

[37] C. Bennema., *Encountering Jesus.* Character Studies in the Gospel of John (Colorado 2009) 70.

[38] Cf. J. D. M. Derrett., *Law in The New Testament* (London, 1970) 237-238; C. S. Keener., *Gospel of John.* A Commentary. 2 Vols. (Grand Rapids, MI 2010) 502.

be reading too much into the text. For this reason, his view does not hold water.

1.2.2.2 τί ἐμοὶ καὶ σοί, γύναι; "what to me and to you, woman?" (John 2, 4)

In his reply, Jesus reacted to the request of his mother, calling her γύναι "woman." He said to her τί ἐμοὶ καὶ σοί, γύναι; "what to me and to you, woman?" This response seems disrespectful to his mother. In this context, Jesus was not being disrespectful to his mother when he called her γύναι, " woman" (John 2,4;19,26). This was an unusual way of greeting a woman (cf. John 4, 21; 20, 13. 15; 8, 10; Matt 15, 28; Luke 13,12; 22, 57; 1 Cor 7, 16). Nevertheless, it was not natural to greet one's mother by calling her "woman" as Jesus did.[39]

According to Brown, calling his mother "woman" was neither a rebuke, an impolite term, nor even an indication of lack of affection. It was simply the usual, polite manner of addressing women by Jesus. It was not a way of reducing or devaluing the mother-son relationship since the mother of Jesus is addressed about four times in John 2, 1-12. His response "woman" points to symbolic meaning, which parallels Matt 15, 28; Luke 13,12; John 4, 21; 8,10; 20,13.[40] Bennema, on the other hand, thinks that this kind of impersonal address by Jesus to his mother may suggest that Jesus is distancing himself from her and rejects any claim she might make about him because of her family ties and relationship.[41]

---

[39] Cf. E. Haenchen., *A Commentary on the Gospel of John*. 2 Vols. (eds. R. W. Funk — U. Busse) (Philadelphia, 1984) 1:173 ; D. R. Beck., *The Discipleship Paradigm*. Readers and Anonymous Characters in the Fourth Gospel (Leiden 1997) 55. Despite the above, we ought to note that, Colwell and Titus, "wrongly suppose that she is no longer Jesus' mother because of his adoption by God in Ch. 1, but this makes little sense of our passage's preference for her relational title over her name, " E. C. Colwell. — E. L. Titus., *The Gospel of the Spirit*. A Study in the Fourth Gospel (New York 1953) 113.

[40] See Brown., *The Gospel*,99.

[41] See Bennema., *Encountering Jesus*, 70-71.

Hoskyns held that the title "woman" is a way of considering the mother of Jesus as "a new Eve as the mother of the new Israel,"[42] "and/or the church."[43] Brown maintained that "some have sought to find symbolic import in the address."[44] Hanhart considered this address "woman" to the mother of Jesus, meaning "representative of Israel."[45]

It is quite difficult to comprehend τί ἐμοὶ καὶ σοί, "what to me and to you" (John 2, 4). Brown holds the view that it is difficult to comprehend the response of Jesus to his mother. He notes that the response τί ἐμοὶ καὶ σοί, "what to me and to you," is a LXX rendering מה לי ולך as in Judges 11, 12; 2 Chron 35, 21; 1 Kgs 17, 18; 2 Kgs 3, 13; 2 Sam 16, 5-13; 2 Sam 19, 23; Joel 4, 4. This Hebrew expression in the Old Testament has two meanings. In the first case, it follows that when one party is unjustly bothering another, the injured party may say: "What to me and to you?" This means: "What subject of discord is there between us"? In this first case, there is hostility. Then, a second case in point is when someone is requested to get involved in a matter that he or she feels is not their business i.e., "How am I involved"? In this second case, there is a sense of disengagement. In these two instances, there is a sense of refusal to get involved. Brown thinks that there is a divergence in the views of people like Schnackenburg and Bulembat. Schnackenburg states that the expression of Jesus above does not mean, "What concern is that of yours and mine?" for the καὶ ought to be understood as a contrasting one that may take on various nuances in accordance with their context and the tone of the voice. It may not necessarily express disassociation or, even

[42] E. C. Hoskyns, "Genesis I-III and St. John's Gospel." *JTS* 21/83 April 1919) 211-212.

[43] A. Feuillet., *Johannine Studies* (trans. E. C. Thomas) (Staten Island, N. Y, 1964)35; T. L. Broodie, *The Gospel according to John*. A Literary and Theological Commentary (New York 1993) 174-175; R. G. Bury., *The Fourth Gospel and the Logos-Doctrine* (Cambridge, 1940) 32, maintains that the "woman is an allegorical symbol for sensation".

[44] See Brown., *The Gospel*, 1:99.

[45] K. Hanhart., "The Structure of John i 35-iv 54", 41.

so to speak, harsh rejection. It may have a milder meaning, such as "Leave me in peace!" or "What would you have me do?"[46] Matand holds that the response of Jesus to his mother must have been an observation.[47] Subsequently, the response of Jesus to his mother is not a rebuke to her. I personally think that Jesus was not disrespecting or disassociating himself from his mother.

1.2.2.3 ἡ ὥρα, "the hour" (John 2, 4)

Jesus said to his mother οὔπω ἥκει ἡ ὥρα μου, "My hour is not yet come" (John 2, 4). Jesus reminded his mother that his hour had not yet come. This expression is an object of debate among scholars. They ask whether this expression is a statement or a rhetorical question. They also ask whether the hour being talked about here concerns the revelation of the glory of Jesus in the sign at Cana of Galilee or it is talking about the hour of the death and the glorification of Jesus. If it is a statement, Jesus is reluctant to be involved in the household crisis. Thus, he said, "My hour has not yet come; the time is not right." What hour? Is it the time for saving the embarrassment of the lack of wine at a wedding feast? Or is it a time for performing miracles? Or for granting favors?

Moreover, if the time has not yet come, why does he perform the sign giving forth the six stone jars of wine?[48] Gregory of Nyssa, Theodore of Mopsuestia, Ephraim, and Tatian, and the modern Catholic exegetes agree to take the expression as a question. Schnackenburg confirms this to be a possible case in grammar. It would be of the sense, "What would you have me do? After all, my hour has already come". Jesus performed the sign just at once. It was carefully prepared by his mother.[49]

---

[46] See Schnackenburg., The *Gospel According to St. John*, 328.
[47] See Bulembat, "Head-Waiter", 67.
[48] See Williams, "The Mother of Jesus at Cana", 689.
[49] See Schnackenburg., The *Gospel According to St. John*, 329.

Barrett holds that this hour of Jesus refers to his death on the cross and his exaltation in glory (cf. John 7, 30; 8, 20). He adds that it is not tenable that in John 2, 4, the "hour" should have a different meaning, like 'the hour for me to supply them wine.'[50] If one interprets this "hour" to mean the exaltation and glorification of Jesus, it will mean that only the hour of his death reveals his glory and the fullness of his messianic gifts. Maybe the signs that he performs are indications of those messianic gifts, such as the eucharist, which is a prefiguration of the age of salvation after the death of Jesus. However, Schnackenburg argues that this is not the sense that this hour gives the reader in this pericope in contrast to the other misunderstandings in John. He concludes that the Cana miracle is meant to portray the character and identity of Jesus as the giver of God's eschatological gifts in the hic et Nunc, "here and now." Also, in this Cana miracle, everything seems to be oriented to the present revelation of Jesus' glory.[51] Bennema maintains that the "hour" in this Cana wedding ceremony refers to the messianic hour. The 'not yet' aspect of this hour is removed from this miracle in Cana of Galilee.[52]

1.2.2.4 ὅ τι ἂν λέγῃ ὑμῖν ποιήσατε, "do whatever he tells you" (John 2, 5)

The next action of the mother of Jesus after encountering her son Jesus was the instruction of the servants at the wedding feast to follow the words of Jesus. She is ready to operate as an agent of mediation. She used her privileged relationship well as a conduit for his patronage. She did not take her son's words as refusal, as others would suggest. She did not even give Jesus an answer. She turned to the servants and instructed them to be ready to respond correctly when Jesus told them to do something. She instructed them, saying ὅ τι ἂν λέγῃ ὑμῖν ποιήσατε, "do whatever he tells you" (John 2,

---

[50] See Barrett, *The Gospel*, 191.

[51] See Schnackenburg., *The Gospel According to St. John*, 330-331.

[52] See Bennema., *Encountering Jesus*, 73.

5). She confidently trusted in the words of her son. This has grown over time through the mother-son relationship. She sensed that he would act even if his response seemed mysterious. Her words of instruction to the servants point to her recognition of the authority of Jesus and demonstrate her expectation that her son would do something to solve the situation at hand.

1.2.2.5 The mother of Jesus turned τοῖς διακόνοις "to the servants" (John 2, 5)

The mother of Jesus left her son and turned τοῖς διακόνοις "to the servants" (John 2, 5). Who are these servants? Some people think these servants were the same as the disciples. However, the text itself does not support this view. This group is impersonal to Jesus, and the text also demonstrates it. According to the text, those present in this group are ἡ μήτηρ τοῦ Ἰησοῦ, "the mother of Jesus" (vv. 1 and 3); οἱ μαθηταὶ αὐτοῦ, "his disciples" (vv. 11-12); ἡ μήτηρ αὐτοῦ, "his mother" (John 2, 5. 12) and οἱ ἀδελφοὶ (αὐτοῦ), "his brothers" (v. 12). All of these people are linked to Jesus except οἱ διάκονοι, "the servants" (John 2, 5).

I think these servants may not be in the same group as the disciples. Barrett holds that the word διάκονοι is not the most natural word for household servants. So, he suggested that it could have been used here because the servants bearing the wine to the guests at the feast recalled the activity of 'deacons' in both Christian and pagan cults.[53] Even when we consider the parallel texts and synoptic gospels where the word servants are used, it is not used to refer directly to the disciples. We can find these in John 12,26; Mark 9,35; 10,43; Matt 20,26;22,13; and 23,11.

1.2.2.6 Importance of the instruction of the Mother of Jesus in John 2, 5

The first sign that Jesus performed in Cana of Galilee is premised on the instruction of the mother of Jesus. Her words to the servants

---

[53] See Barrett, *The Gospel,* 191.

expressed her deep faith in her son Jesus's ability. The expression "whatever he tells you" is the belief that Jesus would answer her request but in ways unexpected. This is the last speech of the mother of Jesus in the gospel of John. It is of great importance because it puts forth the proper attitude of a follower of Jesus, which is the act of obedience to Jesus. It further echoes the words of the divine command in the event of the transfiguration, οὗτός ἐστιν ὁ υἱός μου ὁ ἀγαπητός, ἀκούετε αὐτοῦ, "This is my beloved son, listen to him" (Mark 9, 7). the mother of Jesus stands out as a model of faith and discipleship.[54] Her relationship with Jesus as his mother opens the way for the sign to occur at Cana of Galilee. The mother-son relationship between them played a great role in the performance of the miracle in question. She is notably involved in the beginning of the public ministry of her son Jesus here and later as well at the final scene of his ministry.[55]

1.2.3 Transformative Action (John 2, 6-8)

The transforming action of Jesus is vividly represented in this sub-section of the pericope. He responded to his mother's concern, for his mother had observed that the host family had no wine (John 2, 3). She told Jesus this. John puts it that there were λίθιναι ὑδρίαι ἓξ κατὰ τὸν καθαρισμὸν τῶν Ἰουδαίων, "six stone water pots in accord with the Jewish rite of purification" (v. 6). The number six and the stone pots attract the attention of the reader here. What do they symbolize? Six is one number less than seven. If the number seven symbolized perfection, then six would represent imperfection. This means the Jewish dispensation, with its ceremonial water, was partial and imperfect. Barret argues that no numerical interpretation of the miracle can prove entirely satisfactory

---

[54] See Keener, *Gospel of John*, 506.

[55] Cf. M. Mullins., *The Gospel of John*. A Commentary (Dublin 2003)112.

because Jesus does not introduce a seventh jar.[56] Keener suggests a replacement motif to explain it, holding that the water pots associated with the ritual purity of the Jews are now being used for a new purpose.[57]

The stone pots symbolize and recall the Exod 7, 19 actions of Moses changing to blood the water in the Egyptian stone jars. This use of the stone jars might have come from the Levitical laws of ritual purity (cf. Lev 11, 29-38). Brown notes that the earthen jars could become ritually contaminated and must be broken, but the stone jars could not become impure jars.[58]

Then, the description that the jars are according to the Jewish rite of purification probably symbolizes the conformity to the Judean practice in Galilee and may signify a response to southern polemic Judeans who thought that the Galileans did not keep their high standards of purity.[59] In John 2, 5, the mother of Jesus told the servants to do whatever Jesus told them to do. In this way, she anticipated that Jesus would do something to redress the situation even though she did not precisely know the nature of the action that her son would do. Later, Jesus instructed the servants to fill the jars with water, and they filled them to the brim. This is clearly attested in this pericope saying λέγει αὐτοῖς ὁ Ἰησοῦς· γεμίσατε τὰς ὑδρίας ὕδατος. καὶ ἐγέμισαν αὐτὰς ἕως ἄνω, "Jesus said to them, 'Fill the jars with water.' And they filled them up to the brim" (John 2, 7). This instruction of Jesus makes it impossible to think of John 2, 4 as a refusal to act in response to his mother's request. Before the instruction of Jesus, the servants had already been instructed by the mother of Jesus. Her instruction had made them ready and willing to do whatever Jesus would tell them to do with ease.[60]

---

[56] Cf. Barrett, *The Gospel*, 191.

[57] See Keener., *Gospel of John*, 509.

[58] See Brown, *The Gospel*, 100.

[59] Cf. Brant, *John*, 57.

[60] See Schnackenburg., *The Gospel*, 332.

Jesus gave a second instruction to the servants, and they obeyed. John 2, 8 states: καὶ λέγει αὐτοῖς· ἀντλήσατε νῦν καὶ φέρετε τῷ ἀρχιτρικλίνῳ· οἱ δὲ ἤνεγκαν, "and he said to them, 'now draw some out, and take it to the steward of the feast.' So, they took it." To this second instruction of Jesus, the servants obeyed and did according to the instruction of Jesus without any hesitation. The instruction of the mother of Jesus was not superfluous. The usage of ἀντλήσατε νῦν, "draw out now" (v.8), is interesting. Barrett affirms that it is interesting and attracts attention because ἀντλεῖν in a proper sense is used to mean drawing water from a well (cf. 4, 7.15) and it has been suggested that the servants were instructed to fill the jars from the well first and that the water drawn and brought directly from the well to the wedding feast was transformed in a miraculous way into wine. This was to avoid the difficulty caused by the large quantity of water. It is difficult to agree with this point because it defeats logic, considering the two sequential instructions in vv. 7- 8 in which the first instruction was carried out and finished well, and the second one now comes forth as a consequence and depends on it. He concludes that it is better to comprehend it as 'water become wine' was drawn from the pots, and John probably used the word ἀντλεῖν in a loose sense or as the well of living water.[61]

The servants in question performed the last part of the instruction with equal ease. Jesus instructed them, saying φέρετε τῷ ἀρχιτρικλίνῳ, "Take it to the steward of the feast." (v.8). Moreover, they positively followed the instructions. For οἱ δὲ ἤνεγκαν, "So, they took it" (v. 8). They obediently took the water drawn from the jars to the steward who manages the banquet.[62]

---

[61] Cf. Barrett., *The Gospel*, 192.

[62] Steward, also called headwaiter, comes from a Greek word ἀρχιτρίκλινος . He was the person responsible for the management of the banquet. Cf. M. S. J. Zerwick., — M. A. Grosvenor., *Grammatical Analysis of the Greek New Testament*, 290.

Brown holds that the literature of the Jews gives no exact parallel for the functionary envisaged in John. One may find a parallel in the person who presides at the dinner in Sir 32, 1. In this case, the one who presides is not a servant, not a best man, but a guest chosen to run the affair because he is familiar with the bridegroom.[63] The steward received the water already become wine (v.9).

1.2.4 *The reaction of the steward (John 2, 9-10)*

The process begun in the second unit (John 2, 3-5) gets to be completed here in this section of the pericope. It establishes a reversal motif. The abundance of a better wine reverses the lack of wine. The Steward verified that, indeed, the miracle occurred. John, the evangelist, did not record the action of Jesus; only his words were enough to bring forth the miracle. The steward received the wine brought to him and tasted it. He was so astonished that he called on the attention of the bridegroom because he did not know the origin of this better wine. He told the bridegroom πᾶς ἄνθρωπος πρῶτον τὸν καλὸν οἶνον τίθησιν καὶ ὅταν μεθυσθῶσιν τὸν ἐλάσσω· σὺ τετήρηκας τὸν καλὸν οἶνον ἕως ἄρτι, "every man serves the good wine first; and when men have drunk freely, then the poor wine; but you have kept the good wine until now"(John 2, 10). According to Brown, this kind of custom is not attested in contemporary literature, but it is a shrewd practice peculiar to human nature.[64] The steward's testimony is like an indictment of the bridegroom that the wine provided for his wedding feast was not good. Brand suggests that it is either a challenge to the integrity of the bridegroom, a suggestion that he has been holding out his guests, or just an expression of pleasant surprise.

---

[63] See Brown, *The Gospel*, 100.

[64] Cf. Brown., *The Gospel*, 100.

Nevertheless, by changing water into wine, Jesus saved the steward and the bridegroom from being socially embarrassed due to the lack of wine in the wedding celebration.[65] Even though he called on the attention of the bridegroom, he surprisingly remained silent. He was also ignorant of the origin of this particular wine. He never betrayed his ignorance and never corrected the mistake of the steward.[66]

We have to note that this transformative action of changing water into wine solved the problem of lack of wine by providing an even better quality, which took away public humiliation and disgrace and restored the honor and reputation of the bridegroom, the steward, and the entire family.

1.2.5 Final situation (John 2, 11-12)

The final situation is presented to us through Ταύτην ἐποίησεν ἀρχὴν τῶν σημείων ὁ Ἰησοῦς ἐν Κανὰ τῆς Γαλιλαίας καὶ ἐφανέρωσεν τὴν δόξαν αὐτοῦ, καὶ ἐπίστευσαν εἰς αὐτὸν οἱ μαθηταὶ αὐτοῦ, " this is the first of the signs Jesus did in Cana of Galilee. And he revealed his glory and his disciples believed in him" (John 2,11). This v. 11 presents to us three statements related to each other and are very significant in understanding the objective of this narrative story in John 2, 1-12. The first statement is that what happened was a sign. The Second statement is that the sign reveals the glory of Jesus. Then, the third statement makes us know that this glory of Jesus leads the disciples to believe and to have a deeper understanding of the identity of their master Jesus. We shall look at these under some key elements in John 2,1-12.

This last strophe concluded the narrative with the mention of time, place, and characters as was earlier on done in the initial situation (vv.1-2), hence forming an inclusio and also serving as a transition passage (v.

---

[65] Cf. Brant., John, 58.
[66] Cf. Brant., John, 58.

12)[67] before going forth to the next cardinal event in Jerusalem. This is attested in Μετὰ τοῦτο κατέβη εἰς Καφαρναοὺμ, "after this, they went down to Capernaum" (v. 12). The usage of Μετὰ τοῦτο in this verse serves indicates a transition from one narrative to the next. Therefore, v. 12 is part of John 2, 1-12 since it concludes the pericope in question. It is a conclusion because it repeats the name of place, time, and characters, forming a complete textual unit. The characters introduced earlier in the text are mentioned again in the concluding part. They are mentioned as αὐτὸς καὶ ἡ μήτηρ αὐτοῦ καὶ οἱ ἀδελφοὶ (αὐτοῦ) καὶ οἱ μαθηταὶ αὐτοῦ, "he and his mother and his brothers and his disciples" (v.12). Why are they being mentioned again? They are being mentioned again to bring the narrative to a fitting conclusion.

1.3 Key Elements in John 2, 1-12

In an attempt to comprehend the objectives of the narrative text of John 2,1-12, let us discuss three significant statements found in John 2, 11.

1.3.1 The term "Sign" in John 2, 11.

The mention of the beginning of the signs that Jesus did is in the statement Ταύτην ἐποίησεν ἀρχὴν τῶν σημείων ὁ Ἰησοῦς "this, (the) beginning of the signs Jesus did" (John 2, 11). It should be noted that this construction may have various nuances. It may be translated as "such was the first of the signs that Jesus did." In addition, it may

---

[67] This is supported by Keener, and I agree with him that "2:12 is a transitional paragraph between 2:1-11 and 2:13-22." Keener, *The Gospel*, 517. Barrett holds that this verse permits for a 'geographical transition'. He maintains that "Jesus presumably 'descended' to Capernaum because, on the lake, it was lower in elevation than Cana." C.K. Barrett., *The Gospel of John and Judaism*, 37. Keener adds that John 2, 12 also permits a "chronological transition and provides a necessary historical information about Jesus of Nazareth's residence in Capernaum..." Keener, *The Gospel*, 517.

also be translated as "Jesus did this as his initial sign, literally as a beginning of his signs." In this second translation, the word ἀρχήν is translated as "beginning, origin."[68] Therefore, ἀρχὴν τῶν σημείων, "the beginning of the signs". Barret maintains that using ἀρχήν as referring to the signs may not mean just a mere sign but a "primary sign." [69] This is what Marrow calls the inaugural sign, "the first of his signs," in the series of the signs that will culminate in the raising of Lazarus in chapter 11.[70]

It is worth noting that, after this first sign, the next miracle or sign in Cana was the healing of the official's son in Capernaum, even though, in proxy, it is described as the second sign (John 4, 46 - 54). This healing is considered the second sign in Cana despite Jesus doing other 'signs' in Jerusalem (cf. John 2, 23; 3, 2; 4, 45). Schnackenburg states that this may be so because John follows a σημεῖα-source, and if this is granted then he has exploited it in his own way, selecting and putting emphasis on certain signs, with new and deeper insights on them.[71] Schnackenburg adds that by the fact that John noted explicitly that the miracle that happened at Cana of Galilee is the "first sign" of Jesus, he draws our attention to the beginning of the self-revelation of Jesus before the world, which is meant to be entirely public[72] and for Keener this "makes what he says about it paradigmatic for Jesus' signs in general."[73]

Keener holds that in the prologue of the gospel of John, Jesus is the one who reveals the Father's glory to his disciples just as God revealed his glory to Moses on the mountain. If this sign reveals the character of

[68] Zerwick—Grosvenor., *A Grammatical Analysis*, 290.
[69] Barret., *The Gospel*, 193.
[70] Cf. S. B. Marrow., *The Gospel of John. A Reading*(New York—Mahwah, N. J, 1995)27.
[71] See Schnackenburg., *The Gospel*, 335.
[72] See Schnackenburg., *The Gospel*, 335.
[73] Keener, *The Gospel*, 515.

Jesus by permitting him to show his concern for a bride and groom, it also points to the ultimate glorification of Jesus on the cross.[74]

In the synoptic gospels, the term "miracle" would have been used to describe the amazing and mysterious change from water to Wine by Jesus in John 2, 1-12. In the gospel of John, instead, the word "sign" is used. This attracts our attention and animates our curiosity to know more about it. A "miracle" in the synoptic gospels is a "sign" in the fourth gospel. According to Marrow, this change in terminology is because in the gospel of John and probably nowhere else in the New Testament, everything that Jesus does and says shows us the revelation he brings.[75]

Barrett maintains that the sign we have in John 2, 1-12 is a manifestation of the glory of God to make men believe.[76] Mullins regards this "sign" as a symbolic narrative in which a wedding is considered a prophetic sign. An ordinary event now becomes a means of divine revelation representing something analogous to but greater than itself. It becomes a prophetic אוֹת, "sign," which is σημεῖον, "sign" in the gospel of John. Mullins adds that even though the two concepts are considered "signs," they do not correspond to what the modern world calls signs conventionally, for they are just considered symbols in the understanding of this world of today. This is because a sign points to a reality beyond and outside itself and, of course, one in which it does not participate.[77]

1.3.1.1 The purpose of the sign: Revelation of his glory (John 2, 11)

The statement καὶ ἐφανέρωσεν τὴν δόξαν αὐτοῦ, "and he revealed his glory" (v. 11) brings forth the purpose of the sign done by Jesus in John 2,1-12. This verse states that the purpose of this sign was to reveal

---

[74] See Keener, *The Gospel*, 515.

[75] Cf. Marrow., *The Gospel of John*, 28.

[76] Cf. Barrett., *The Gospel*, 193.

[77] See Mullins, *The Gospel of John*, 113.

his glory. Brown maintains that for John, the authentic glory of Jesus is revealed only in "the hour."[78]

John 2, 11 is to be understood as referring to a partial revelation of his glory. It could also be understood as being part of the capsulizing of the training of the followers of Jesus, where their entire career, including their sight of the glory of the resurrection, is foreshadowed.[79] It is worth noting that the combination of δόχα, "glory," and φανερόω, "to reveal or to manifest," does not allow for an immediate conclusion that it always means the divine radiance, the heavenly "brightness" which is penetrating the veil of the flesh. However, the choice of φανερόω to express the experience of faith is important. Here, there is no transfiguration, no temporary elevation of Jesus to a heavenly way of being. This glory that Jesus possesses, and reveals should be comprehended as the effect of the divine and heavenly glory he already had before the world's creation. It may be incorrect to restrict the revelation of the glory of Jesus at the wedding at Cana of Galilee to his divine and miraculous power.[80] The glory of Jesus would be revealed or manifested in great measure in his cross, resurrection, and exaltation. Prior to this, though, it is important to note that every step along the path of his ministry counts because each of that step anticipates that δόχα, "glory."[81]

In a larger context of the fourth gospel, Keener maintains that "the signs suggest that Jesus is one greater than Moses, and Jesus, God's agent, joins God the Father as the supreme object of Salvific, revelatory vision, and knowledge."[82]

---

[78] This is because we see in John 7, 39 that during the ministry Jesus had not yet been glorified. This is why v. 11 of this pericope needs to be taken as a partial revelation or manifestation of his glory being talked about here.

[79] Cf. Brown, *The Gospel*,100-101.

[80] See Schnackenburg., *The Gospel*, 336.

[81] D. A. Carson., *The Gospel According to John* (Grand Rapids, MI 1991)175.

[82] Cf. Keener, *The Gospel*,279.

1.3.1.2 The usefulness of the glory of Jesus revealed in John 2, 11

From the statement καὶ ἐπίστευσαν εἰς αὐτὸν οἱ μαθηταὶ αὐτοῦ, "and his disciples (they) believed in him" (v. 11) we note that the usefulness of glory of Jesus revealed in Cana of Galilee at a wedding feast to his disciples was that ἐπίστευσαν εἰς αὐτὸν "they believed in him" (v. 11). This glory was not seen by all who witnessed the sign. For example, the servants saw the sign but not the glory of Jesus. The disciples perceived the glory of Jesus behind the sign through faith. This made them commit their faith in him. Barrett holds that πιστεύειν means that the disciples believed because of the revelation of the glory of Jesus in this first sign he did at Cana of Galilee. Even though the "hour" had not yet come for the revelation of his glory, Jesus did give a partial and, so to speak, a preliminary manifestation of his glory in order that they might believe. This pericope concludes with seeing and believing of the disciples of Jesus as a supreme sign through which faith becomes a wider option (John 20, 29).[83] Belief is of much significance. This sign was meant to lead the disciples of Jesus to believe and, in this way, bring to completion their vocation to discipleship and living a life of witness.

1.4 Setting of John 2,1-12

The setting of the sign is very significant to the narrative of John. This section shall focus on place , day, and the wedding custom. Here below, we begin by examining the place Cana of Galilee.

1.4.1 Place: Cana of Galilee (John 2, 1)

In section 1.2.1.3 the reason why Cana of Galilee was mentioned was discussed. It is a place where Jesus performed the sign. This location

---

[83] Cf. Barrett., *The Gospel*, 193-194.

is mentioned in John 2, 1. 11. Braun says, "The mention of Cana frames this pericope, bracketing it (2,1.11)."[84] Keener, Derrett, Mackowski, and Brown maintain that "scholars have favored especially two sites, kefar-Kenna, and Khirbet-Qanah, as the ancient site of John's Cana; more evidence supports the claim for the latter. Despite recent traditions supporting Kefar-Kenna, older sources support Khirbet-Qanah".[85] The description of this locality by Josephus also "tend to support Khirbet-Qanah."[86] Keener notes that both of these places required a "reasonable walk from Nazareth" and consequently this gives us the reason as to why the family of Jesus would have known the family of the groom. For instance, Kefar-Kenna is 3.5 miles northeast of Nazareth, and Khirbet-Qanah is 9 miles north of Nazareth.[87] This place, Cana, mentioned in the text, may serve as "historical reminiscence."[88]

1.4.2 The third day (John 2, 1)

Keener holds that John has "tied the two major pericopes of John 2 together with a literary inclusio around the key phrase 'three days'(John 2, 1.19)."[89] The third day mentioned in John's gospel is quite puzzling to many scholars. There is no indication of a particular day in which Jesus

---

[84] F. M., Braun., *Jean le théologien et son évangile dans l'église ancienne*. Études bibliques (Paris 1959)16.

[85] Cf. Keener, *The Gospel*,495; J. D. M. Derrett., *Law in the New Testament*, 235, n.2; R. M. Mackowski., "Scholars' Qanah: A Re-examination of the Evidence in Favor of Khirbet-Qanah." *BZ* 23 (1979) 282-283; R. E. Brown., *The Gospel According to John*, 1:98.

[86] Cf. Brown., *John*, 1:98.

[87] Cf. Keener., *The Gospel*, 496.

[88] Infact, "perhaps Nathanael's (who may also represent the connection with the groom's family, since he was from there (John 21, 2) — and as a literary cue prefiguring the sign of John 4, 46-54..." and also mention of "Cana of Galilee (John 2, 1; 4, 46) addressed the contrast implied between the positive reception of Jesus (2, 13—25; 5, 16)". See Cf. Keener., *The Gospel*, 496.

[89] Keener, *The Gospel*,496.

and his disciples did arrive for the wedding. Weddings took seven days in normal circumstances. A good example was the marriage of Tobias, which was celebrated for seven days with great festivity (cf. Tob 11,19). However, there is also a case of a wedding feast and celebration for 14 days. This was an exceptional one that happened because of the deliverance of Sarah (cf. Tob 8, 19-20).

Keener maintains that the wedding itself was celebrated on the third day.[90] According to Michaels, If we begin with "the next day" found in John 1, 29, our "third day" will be the sixth day. The "six days" have been considered to be the "historical reminiscence"[91] while to "others as a means of paralleling the wedding with the lamb announcement."[92] However, other people think it is "the six or seven days of a new creation"[93] or considered "as a parallel with the revelation at Sinai" (Exod 24, 16)[94] This text in question does not mean "the third day of the week: virgins were married on the fourth day, and widows on the fifth."[95]

Why is this day being called "the third day?" There have been some attempts to think of "a parallel with the third day in the Pentecost-Sinai tradition."[96] Flusser, Dunn, and Noack argue that "if John intended the wine to symbolize the antiquity of the Pentecost-Sinai connection itself

---

[90] Cf. Keener, *The Gospel*, 496.

[91] J. R. Michaels, *John* (GNC; San Francisco 1984)11.

[92] J. C. Kirby, *Ephesians*. Baptism and Pentecost: An Inquiry into the Structure and Purpose of the Epistle to the Ephesians (Montreal 1968)152-153.

[93] J. E. Bruns., *The Art and Thought of John* (New York 1969)25; D. A. Carson., *The Gospel according to John* (Grand Rapids, MI 1991) 168 (He suggests a Sabbath image, but a Jewish reader would not see a wedding then); W.F. Hambly., "Creation and Gospel: A Brief Comparison of Genesis 1,1-2,4 and John 1,1-2,12.", *SE* 5 (1968) 70-71; T. Barosse., "The Seven Days of the New Creation in St. John's Gospel", *CBQ* 21 (1959) 508-514.

[94] T. F. Glasson, *Moses in the Fourth Gospel* (SBT 40; Naperville, 1963) 71.

[95] Keener, *The Gospel*, 496.

[96] Moloney "finds an allusion to four days of preparation preceding the final three days before the revelation on Sinai (Exod 19:1-10)", see F. J. Moloney., *Belief in the Word*. Reading the Fourth Gospel — John 1—4 (Minneapolis 1993) 58.

remains in question."[97] John himself never made any link between his "pneumatology" and "Pentecost." This is because the principal linkage, " as in 7, 37-39, "is with sukkoth and an emphasis on the Spirit 'dwelling' among believers."[98] Biblically speaking, the idea of "God coming on Sinai on the third day makes sense (Exod 19, 11.16), but even more likely in the Johannine context...would be an allusion to the biblical tradition of resurrection on the third day" (Hos 6, 2). Nevertheless, it is not easy to link this concept of the "third day" with Sinai when this "expression" is very "common in Scripture."[99]

The expression "third day "was commonly used when one would want to deal with "a short period of time" (see Gen 22, 4; 31, 22; 34, 25; 40, 20; 42, 18; Lev 7, 17-18; 19, 6-7; Num 7, 24; 19, 12.19; 29, 20; 31, 19). Carson maintains that John the evangelist might be using the expression "third day" to mean two days "after the events he had just narrated, thus allowing some time for Jesus to travel."[100] There is a view that the "third day" was a "frequent Biblical idiom" used to mean " the day after tomorrow" or "before yesterday"(cf. Exod 19,11.15.16; 1 Sam 20,12).[101] John might have also intended to use this expression of "third day" to give theological importance in link with the tradition of the resurrection of Jesus on the third day.[102]

---

[97] D. Flusser., *Judaism and the Origins of Christianity* (Jerusalem 1988) 48; J. D. G. Dunn., *Baptism in the Holy Spirit*. A Re-examining of the New Testament Teaching on the Gift of the Spirit in relation to Pentecostalism Today (SBT 15; London 1970) 48; B. Noack.," The Day of the Pentecost in Jubilees, Qumran, and Acts", *Annual of the Swedish Theological Institute* 1 (1962) 89; C. F. Sleeper., "Pentecost and Resurrection", *JBL* 84 (1965) 390.

[98] Keener, *The Gospel*,497.

[99] For instance, "the third day may refer to resurrection" (Hos. 6, 2); "the revelation" (Exod. 19, 16); Jonah 2, 1, "the time of return from exile" (Ezra 8, 32);"or Abraham's merit" (Gen 22, 4).

[100] D. A. Carson., *The Gospel according to John*, 167.

[101] See Keener, *The Gospel*,497.

[102] Cf. T. L. Brodie., *The Gospel according to John*, 131; R. A. Culpepper., *Anatomy of the Fourth Gospel*, 193.

1.4.3 Wedding custom (John 2, 2-3a)

According to the Greeks, marriage feasts were inevitable in any marriage. These feasts could even be used in Court of law to prove that a legal marriage was done. The wedding feasts would be the evidence to show that it was not just a mere cohabitation, but legal marriage was contracted. [103] In the Jewish wedding customs, an emphasis is put on the joyous "celebration at wedding feasts" (cf. Jer 33, 11; John 3, 29; Rev 19, 7 ; Mark 2, 19). These joyous celebrations were done in contrast to its "social antithesis, mourning especially for a death" (cf. 1 Macc 1, 27; 9, 39-41; 3 Mac 4, 6; Jer 7, 34; 16, 9; 25, 10; Joel 2, 16; Rev 18, 23). Music was also important to the wedding custom, especially in the "banquet" scenery (cf. Luke 7,32; Matt 11,17; "for banquets in general" (Sir 35, 3-4).

Keener adds that the marriage procession, rejoicing, and celebrating with the groom or bride at their wedding ceremony was part of the wedding custom. Joy was a very significant aspect of it, too. To allow for this joy at a wedding, the rabbis exempted the "groomsman and his wedding party" from the festal obligations like the feast of Sukkoth and even the tefillin. However, they were not exempted from reciting the Shema. The patronage of God over the wedding of Adam and Eve was emphasized as "a model" of the significance of the Wedding.[104] Brown notes that the celebrations of the wedding "lasted seven days."[105]

It is worth noting that "a wealthy person might throw a public banquet for a whole city at a wedding" (Luke 14, 21; Matt 22, 3-10). The people who were not so wealthy could also invite as many people as possible. Weddings attract so many people. The invitation was extended

---

[103] See C. S. Keener., "Marriage", *Dictionary of New Testament*, 685—686 on wedding customs. Feasting was one important aspect of the life of the society and even in the Bible hence attested by Matthew 22 and Rev. 19, 9. descriptions of it.

[104] See Keener, *The Gospel*,498.

[105] R. E. BROWN., *The Gospel according to John*, 1:97-98.

to one's "friend ... his wife, children, hired man", and if need be, even "his dog."[106] According to Keener, in a context where a person did not like the "host," he or she would still accept the invitation, which was "socially appropriate."[107]

Calvin held that Jesus was invited with his mother because "they were probably near relatives." The wedding in John 2, 1-12 took place in Cana of Galilee. Cana and Nazareth were not close to each other, even if they were a walking distance away. The family of Jesus "were at most acquaintances, and Jesus' disciples were even less likely known directly to the groom...it was natural for a scholar to be invited to a wedding...orators could offer speeches at weddings...was praiseworthy to extend hospitality to sages and their disciples"[108] prior to the time Jesus did the signs (John 2, 11) he was believed to have had already some disciples (John 2, 2; 1, 35-51).

Wine was an important drink in the wedding custom. Wine was not simply drunk to purify water, as some people have claimed. It was seen as a helpful medicine by the Greeks and Romans.[109] However, the wine was diluted because the wine which was not diluted was considered dangerous. There were moments when "men competed in heroic drinking parties, sometimes with disastrous results" (cf. Isa 5, 22). In Judaism, "drunkenness" was not viewed favorably (Eccl 10, 17)[110]. The people who were responsible for the festivities of the Jews, like weddings, might have worked hard to minimize the behavior of drunkenness. Those who became drunk were dismissed. Alcohol could make one lose control. This could lead to military defeat (1 Esd 3, 17-24; Jdt 13,15).

---

[106] See Keener, *The Gospel*,499.

[107] Infact it was any act of "nonattendance was offensive". C.S. Keener., *A Commentary on the Gospel of Matthew*, 519-520.

[108] Keener, *The Gospel*, 499.

[109] Cf. M. Cary — T. J. Haarhoff, *Life and Thought in the Greek and Roman World* (London ⁴1946) 95.

[110] See C. S. Keener., *Paul, Women and Wives*. Marriage and Women's Ministry in the Letters of Paul (Peabody 1992) 261-263.

Wine was necessary for any well-planned and organized public celebration. It was part of daily life in the ancient Mediterranean and even Palestine. This is probably why in Jewish feasts wine was necessary.[111] Jeremias held the view that wine was considered "helpful for dancing... and dancing was integral to celebrations (Luke 15, 25; John 8, 12-20), including weddings (Cf. Jer 31, 13)."[112] Keener maintained that wine was so important that even an act of importing it from some remote areas for the performance of kiddush and Habdalah was considered a praiseworthy act by some rabbinic texts.[113]

According to Judge Stambaugh and David, wedding gifts were also necessary. In the Greco-Roman mindset, "the principle of reciprocity governed wedding invitations and all social obligations (Luke 14, 12)."[114] In fact, Malina and Rohrbaugh add that this wedding gift was so important that it was even "considered" as a loan, except when the gift was just a wine. This wedding gift was "recoverable in a court of law."[115] This is probably why Derrett suggested that the words "they have no wine" of Jesus's mother should be considered an accusation.[116] In the Jewish culture, people were meant to eat and leave food leftovers in wedding celebrations. It was uncommon to have food run out at these functions[117].

---

[111] See Keener, *The Gospel*, 501.

[112] Cf. J. Jeremias, *The Parables of Jesus* (New York ²1972) 161.

[113] Cf. Keener, *The Gospel*, 501.

[114] E. A. Judge., *Rank and Status in the World of the Caesars and St. Paul*. Broadhead Memorial Lecture 1981 (Christchurch, N. Z 1982) 26; J. E. Stambaugh — L. B. David, *The New Testament in Its Social Environment* (LEC 2; Philadelphia, 1986) 63-64.

[115] B. J. Malina., — L. R. Richard., *Social Science Commentary on the Gospel of John* (Minneapolis 1998) 70.

[116] Cf. J. D. M. Derrett., *Law in The New Testament*, 237-238.

[117] Probably "there is an implicit contrast between the original host of John 2, 3 and the host (Jesus) of 6, 13, since in both cases Jesus must multiply the resources available to sustain a crowd." Keener, *The Gospel*, 503.

1.5 Intratextuality and Intertextuality

1.5.1 Intratextuality

The first sign of Jesus in John 2,1-12 points to the glory of Jesus. If we look at it from a sacramental perspective and consider the fact that the sacrament is also just a sign that points to a reality beyond itself and in which it does not participate, we can say that the wine that Jesus brought forth miraculously parallels the bread in John 6. This wine and the bread will then constitute the Eucharistic symbol of bread and wine. The meaning of the sign in the gospel of John points to the authority of Jesus and his unity with the Father (cf. 5, 19-30; 10, 37-38; 14, 10-11).

In John 2, 11, signs play a great role in leading the disciples to faith in Jesus. This idea of sign leading to faith is developed further in the Gospel of John 20, 30-31 where "signs" are "a focal point in the fourth gospel, calling one to faith. Signs-faith is inadequate in the Fourth Gospel, but it is a valid step to full discipleship."[118]

The faith of the mother of Jesus (John 2, 3-5) was so moving that we could compare it with the great and moving faith of Mary, who was the sister of Lazarus and Martha (John 11, 32-33). The mother of Jesus approached and requested Jesus as a miracle worker, and Jesus, replying to her, responded like the Lord of his mother. His response can be paralleled

---

[118] Keener continues to explain here while citing texts of scripture which develops this theme of "sign" and how it leads to faith within the Gospel of John. He notes that signs may lead to faith in the contexts where "signs produce faith of unworthy people" (John 2, 23). Further, in other situation where the theme of sign is developed with the fact of complaint of Jesus. Thus, "Jesus complains about those who require signs for faith"(John 4, 48). This notion of sign does not end there, we also see the "crowds demand a sign before faith, although they have already received signs"(6,30). In addition, "many members of the crowds believed Jesus because of his signs"(John 7,31); "people are believing because of Jesus' signs" (John 11, 47-48) and "the crowds refused to believe despite Jesus's signs (though even some rulers did believe secretly— John 12, 42" (John 12, 37). For these, See Keener, *The Gospel*, 276-277.

to John 7, 6-8, in which he did what was asked of him, showing that he depends on the divine timing.[119]

1.5.2 Intertextuality

The instruction ὅ τι ἄν λέγῃ ὑμῖν ποιήσατε, "do whatever he tells you" (John 2, 5) given by the mother of Jesus to the servants has its parallel in the words of Pharaoh πορεύεσθε πρὸς Ιωσηφ καὶ ὃ ἐὰν εἴπῃ ὑμῖν ποιήσατε, "go to Joseph and do whatever he tells you" (Gen 41, 55). This parallel highlight the significance of obeying Jesus, especially his word. Just as Joseph did, Jesus will provide abundantly in times of need, such as that lack of wine at the wedding ceremony of Cana of Galilee.[120]

The event of the wedding feast happened on τῇ ἡμέρᾳ τῇ τρίτῃ, "on the third day" (2,1). The mentioning of "on the third day" here echoes the Sinai background, especially the Torah's giving on the third day (Exod 19, 16) and the abundant wine on the third day, which alludes to the messianic age. Jesus revealed himself as the messiah uniquely and especially as the son of man come down from heaven, as the son of God sent by the Father and united with him. It is not the wine in itself in contrast to the water that makes the signs. The wine is the gift of Jesus, a sign that hails from him and points to him. It is given at the end. It is of a better quality than the prior wine. It is, thus, the eschatological gift of the Messiah.[121]

The words of the mother of Jesus, "Do whatever he tells you" (John 2, 5), indicate the right attitude of obedience to Jesus that an authentic disciple ought to have. This call to obey the words of Jesus echoes the divine command at the event of the transfiguration. God said in the transfiguration, "This is my beloved Son; listen to him" (Mark 9, 7).

---

[119] Haenchen, *John*, 1:173; 2:3; Barrett, *John*, 191; Michaels, *John*, 30-31.
[120] Cf. C.S. Keener., *Gospel of John*, 509.
[121] See Schnackenburg., *The Gospel*, 337-338.

The concept of sign we find in John 2,11 is also common in the Old Testament. In the Old Testament, it is called אוֹת, "sign." The term "sign" refers to both normal and supernormal events, demonstrating the truth of the word of God through his prophet (Exod 3, 12; 1 Sam 10, 1-9. This authenticates the prophet himself (Cf. Exod 4, 1-9). It also refers to events related to the eschatological future (Cf. Isa. 7, 10-16).

The faith of the mother of Jesus demonstrated by her in 2, 3b-5 was so strong just like the faith of the Old Testament persons ("Jacob in Gen 32, 26-30; Moses in Exod 33, 12-34,9; the Shunammite woman in 2 Kgs 4,14-28; Elisha in 2 Kgs 2,2.4.6.9; and Elijah in 1 Kgs 18,36-37,41-46") also " in the Gospel Tradition" (Mark 5,27-34 which has a woman who was not allowed by ritual to "touch the teacher" (Lev 15, 25-27); 7, 24-30; 10,46-52; Matt 8,7-13.

1.6 The Mother of Jesus[122] at the wedding at Cana of Galilee (John 2, 1-12).

The character of the mother of Jesus is seen in her expression of the self with great faith in her son (John 2, 3b-5).[123] From the above study, we see that the mother of Jesus is exemplary because her roles stand out as good examples for the mothers and all of us to learn from. She is the model of

---

[122] The mother of Jesus is the main character whose role is being studied. It ought to be noted that, In dealing with character study, we understand that the characters are the dramatic persons in the story. They reveal themselves in their speech especially through what they say and how they say it. They also reveal themselves through their actions, clothing, in their gestures and posture. For this see J. L. Resseguie., *Narrative Criticism of the New Testament*. An introduction (Grand Rapids 2005) 121.

[123] Regarding the faith of the mother of Jesus(John 2, 3b-5), Keener adds that her faith became a catalyst for the action of Jesus. Her request to him showed both respect for Jesus and demonstrated a faith that never relented. She believed that he would "do what She" requested. See Keener., *Gospel of John*, 501.

faith[124] , given that she expressed to her son the problem of the lack of wine in the host family (John 2, 3). She instructed the servants, preparing them to practice the word Jesus would tell them to do (John 2, 5). She is observant and takes the initiative because, in the text, no one told her that the family had no wine. She observed the facts on the ground and took the first step to find a solution to the identified problem. She went and talked about it with her son Jesus (John 2, 3). She was convinced that her son would do something to solve the situation.[125] The mother of Jesus organized the servants to respond positively even without any expressed agreement between her and her son. She led the dialogue. She organized all the protagonists to collaborate in the performance of the sign to act and play their part. She did so by instructing the servants to do what Jesus would ask them to do. She is an instructor. She appears two times in the gospel of John (John 2, 1-12 and 19, 25-27), but in John 6, she is only mentioned in passing. Her presence frames the public ministry of Jesus, her son.[126]

As we noticed before, the narrator did not give her a personal name. Keener notes, "Whereas the other gospels name Jesus' mother, John does not."[127] She is addressed as the "mother[128] and woman."[129] Maybe John the Evangelist followed the patterns attested in the ancient texts, whereby writers would not call an important person or character by a personal

---

[124] Keener notes that the mother of Jesus gives us "a positive model of faith, even if 2:4 shows that her faith, though positive, is uninformed from within the story world", Keener., *Gospel of John*, 504.

[125] Keener., *Gospel of John*, 501.

[126] Cf. Williams, R. H., "The Mother of Jesus at Cana. A Social- Science Interpretation of John 2, 1-12" *CBQ* 59 (1997) 679.

[127] Keener, *The Gospel*, 501. John is not trying to "avoid confusion with another Mary" (John 11, 1-2,19-20.28.31-32.45;12,3) "since he does not mention others including Mary Magdalene, who could not be Mary of Bethany" (John 19, 25; 20,1.11.16.18; cf. John 11,1); "he also mentions other namesakes" (14, 22).

[128] Here the narrator calls her "the mother of Jesus" (John 2,1.3); "his mother" (John 2, 5.12).

[129] She is also called "woman" in John 2, 4.

name but as "the mother of so-and-so."[130] Her initial words, "They have no wine" (v.3)[131] , and the first response of Jesus, "What is this to me and to you, woman" (v.4), seem to be just a simple statement of fact[132]. Interestingly, the mother of Jesus asked for a favor not for herself but for the bridegroom's family, who were about to be socially embarrassed and humiliated.[133] She put herself in their situation of lack of wine and humiliation in a tenuous position. She participates in the social status and prestige of Jesus because of her relationship with him as his mother. She took upon herself the problem of someone else and made it her problem. Any refusal to solve the problem would also be a refusal of her attempt to function as a broker on his behalf.[134]

---

[130] T. W. Martin., "Assessing the Johannine Epithet 'the Mother of Jesus", *CBQ* 60(1998) 63-73. However, Beck "argues that Greco-Roman literature rarely leaves important characters anonymous; but in Hebrew texts, see the women of 1 Kings 17, 9-24; 2 Kgs 4," D. R. Beck., *The Discipleship Paradigm*, 17-26. He continues to explain that even though someone may think that the names of other men(John 4, 46; 5, 5; 9, 1) and women (John 4, 7) were not passed on in the tradition, "few Christians could be unaware of the name of Jesus' mother once Mark(and more so Matthew and Luke)was in circulation; John may be independent, but that would not make him unaware of information that must have circulated widely in the early church." See Beck, *The Discipleship Paradigm,*132-136.

[131] This apparently neutral statement of the mother of Jesus could be understood as a linguistic strategy of indirectness where without making an explicit request, she presumes that as a result of her relationship with Jesus as his mother he would hear the implied request. The response of Jesus affirmed the correctness of her presumption. He heard her implicit request. See M. L. Coloe., "The Mother of Jesus. A Woman Possessed", *Character Studies in the Fourth Gospel:* Narrative Approaches to seventy Figures in John (ed. S. A. Hunt) (Tübingen 2013) 204-205.

[132] This is probably because Derrett holds the view that, the mother of Jesus "would have been in a position in the house to have known about the shortage of wine", Derrett, *Law*, 235.

[133] Safrai noted that " the groom was facing a potential social stigma that could make him the talk of his guests for years to come. Wine was indispensable to any properly hosted public celebration" Safrai, "Home,"747.

[134] Cf. Williams, "The Mother of Jesus at Cana. A Social- Science Interpretation of John 2:1-12", 688.

In the end, Jesus went to Capernaum with his mother, his brethren, and his disciples (v. 12). She continued to accompany Jesus in his ministry already inaugurated in her presence and with her contribution as a major player in the entire event of transformation. Despite the tension in Jesus's remarks to his mother at Cana of Galilee, he accepted her as seen in the synoptic gospels (cf. Matt 12, 46-50; Mark 3, 31-35; Luke 8, 19-21)[135].

1.7 Conclusion

This first chapter has done an exegetical study of John 2,1-12. It focused on the mother of Jesus at the wedding of Cana of Galilee (John 2, 1-12). Here, John begins his presentation of the public ministry of Jesus with a narrative of the pericope concerned with the first sign of Jesus. This episode reveals the glory of Jesus and the role of the mother of Jesus as an intercessor and model of trusting faith in Jesus. It further reveals to us that the mother of Jesus is a commander (John 2, 5), an organizer , a problem solver, initiative taker, She is a good and conscious companion to the son in times of celebrations and indeed a woman who never takes offense.[136] This text led the disciples to believe in Jesus (John 2, 11). It also invites the reader to believe in Jesus. This pericope also highlights the last words of the mother of Jesus and the importance of obedience to the word of Jesus.

This chapter has exegetically studied and presented preliminary matters: context of John 2, 1-12 (the immediate context of John 2, 1-12; the global context of John 2, 1-12), delimitation of John 2, 1-12, textual criticism of John 2, 1-12, text and translation of John 2,1-12, narrative

---

[135] Cf. Williams, "The Mother of Jesus at Cana. A Social- Science Interpretation of John 2:1-12", 690.

[136] For example, in John 2,4 Jesus called his mother "woman" and she never bothered about it.

structure of John 2,1-12 according to Matand, brief explanation of the concentric structure of Matand, narrative analysis of John 2, 1-12 : initial situation presented in John 2, 1-2 (Καὶ τῇ ʽἡμέρᾳ τῇ τρίτῃ , "and on the third day" in John 2,1; γάμος ἐγένετο, "a wedding took place" in John 2,1; ἐν Κανὰ τῆς Γαλιλαίας, "in Cana of Galilee" in John 2,1), main characters were introduced in John 2, 1-2 as being ἡ μήτηρ τοῦ Ἰησοῦ, "the mother of Jesus" (2,1) and οἱ μαθηταὶ αὐτοῦ, "his disciples" (John 2, 2). It discussed also: the action of the mother of Jesus in an attempt to solve the problem in John 2, 3-5 : οἶνον οὐκ ἔχουσιν, "they have not wine" (John 2, 3); τί ἐμοὶ καὶ σοί, γύναι; "what to me and to you, woman?" (John 2, 4); ἡ ὥρα , "the hour" (John 2, 4); ὅ τι ἂν λέγῃ ὑμῖν ποιήσατε, "do whatever he tells you" (John 2, 5); the mother of Jesus turned τοῖς διακόνοις "to the servants"(John 2, 5) and the importance of the instruction of the Mother of Jesus in John 2, 5. It also handled the transformative action (John 2, 6-8), the reaction of the steward (John 2, 9-10), and final situation (John 2, 11-12). It continued and discussed the key elements in John 2, 1-12 by looking at the term "Sign" in John 2, 11 (the purpose of the sign: revelation of his glory as in John 2, 11; the usefulness of the glory of Jesus revealed in John 2, 11), setting of John 2,1-12 by considering the place to be Cana of Galilee as presented in John 2, 1; the third day as in John 2, 1; and the wedding custom in John 2, 2-3a. We also studied the intratextual and intertextual links that this pericope has with other texts of both the Old and New Testaments. We concluded with the mother of Jesus at the wedding at Cana of Galilee (John 2, 1-12) and the study was concluded.

It is worth noting that in John 2,1-12, the narrator has presented to us the first sign performed by Jesus at a wedding feast of Cana of Galilee. His deeds are generally called "signs" in the gospel of John. These signs are not the end in themselves but indicators of the work of God in the world. Thompson maintains that these signs reveal the identity of Jesus "as the messiah and son of God".[137] This narrative text presenting the "first" of the series of signs that Jesus performed serves to inaugurate the public ministry of Jesus in the gospel of John. This first sign shows divine presence and intervention in human suffering and complex situations. It reveals the glory and the identity of Jesus. This pericope also has revealed to us that the mother of Jesus, by nature, is caring, practical, observant, shows initiative, is empathetic, and plays a great role in the revelation of Jesus. It was through her request to Jesus that the public, messianic, and Christological ministry of Jesus was launched in John 2, 1-12 by this first sign. She is a catalyst that led to the belief of the disciples in Jesus.[138] This text points to the significance of obedience as the mother of Jesus said to the servants, "Do whatever he tells you" (John 2, 5). This was the last speech that the mother of Jesus made in the gospel of John. This brings the importance of the "spoken word" in the old and new order. By his word, Jesus spoke to the servants, and the "sign" of water changed into wine was done. This is also true of the second sign at Cana (John 4, 46-54). We remember here the old order which came to exist by the power of the creative word of God in Gen 1, 1-2.3.

---

[137] Cf. M. M. Thompson., *John. A Commentary* (NTL; Louisville 2015)64. Indeed, the disciples acknowledged the identity of Jesus as messiah (John 1,45.49).

[138] Bennema, *Encountering Jesus*, 75.

CHAPTER II

The mother of Jesus
at the foot of the cross
(John 19, 25-27)

2.0 Introduction

This second chapter will be dedicated to the exegesis of John 19, 25-27 with a focus on the mother of Jesus at the foot of the cross (John 19, 25-27). This chapter will be introduced, and immediately we proceed to look at the preliminary matters such as context of John 19, 25-27, delimitation of John 19, 25-27, an issue of exegetical interpretation in John 19, 25 (two women, three women, four women), text and translation of John 19, 25-27, narrative structure and analysis: plot of John 19, 25-27 (Initial situation in John 19, 25; Complication in John 19, 26a; Transformative action in John 19, 26b-27a; and then, resolution and final situation in John 19, 27b). This chapter will also discuss key elements in John 19, 25-27 by considering and studying the women by the cross (John 19, 25); γύναι, "woman" (John 19, 26a); and ἀπ᾽ ἐκείνης τῆς ὥρας "from that hour" (John 19, 27). It will also study Setting of John 19, 25 – 27, intratextual and Intertextual connections with other texts within the Old and New Testaments, the mother of Jesus and the beloved disciple at the foot of the Cross and a conclusion will be given.

2.1 Preliminary Matters

2.1.1 Context of John 19, 25-27

Keener holds that this pericope is placed within the context of "the passion and death of Jesus according to John" (18-19).[139] This is narrowed down to "the crucifixion and the death of Jesus" (19, 17-30). The crucifixion and the death of Jesus occurred at the cross. John 19, 25-27 brings us a narrative of what happened at the foot of the cross in a more specific sense of the word.[140] Wahlde places our text in the context of " the crucifixion, the events at the cross, the death of Jesus (19, 16b-30)."[141] Moloney places this "Johannine passion account" in the context of John 18, 1–19, 42.[142]

2.1.2 Delimitation of John 19, 25-27

The text we are dealing with is John 19, 25-27. This narrative unit begins at v. 25 and ends with v. 27.[143] The previous narrative unit ended with v. 24 εἶπαν οὖν πρὸς ἀλλήλους· μὴ σχίσωμεν αὐτόν, ἀλλὰ λάχωμεν περὶ αὐτοῦ τίνος ἔσται· ἵνα ἡ γραφὴ πληρωθῇ [ἡ λέγουσα]· διεμερίσαντο τὰ ἱμάτιά μου ἑαυτοῖς καὶ ἐπὶ τὸν ἱματισμόν μου ἔβαλον κλῆρον. Οἱ μὲν

---

[139] Keener generally places this subunit within the "passion(John 18, 1 - 19, 42)" and in a specific sense within the unit dealing with the presence of the disciple whom Jesus loved (19:17-30). Keener, *The Gospel According to John*, 1067.

[140] J. Zumstein., "The Mother of Jesus and the Beloved Disciple: How a New Family is Established under the Cross", 641.

[141] Cf. U. C. von Wahlde., "John", 1436.

[142] Cf. J. Moloney., "John", 1107.

[143] In Beasley-Murray i note that, v.24 concludes the prior narrative unit on the division of the clothes of Jesus in John 19, 23-24. Following it then, comes a new narrative unit (John 19, 25-27) which begins with v.25 and ends with v.27 describing how Jesus gives his mother to the beloved disciple. After this, comes another new narrative unit (19, 28-30) beginning with v.28 and ending at v.30 with a focus on the death of Jesus. Cf. G. R. Beasley-Murray., *John*. (WBC 36; Texas, ²1999) 347-353.

οὖν στρατιῶται ταῦτα ἐποίησαν, "So, they said to one another, "Let us not tear it, but cast lots for it to see whose it shall be." This was to fulfill the Scripture, "They parted my garments among them, and for my clothing they cast lots."[144] A new narrative unit begins with Εἰστήκεισαν δὲ παρὰ τῷ σταυρῷ τοῦ Ἰησοῦ ἡ μήτηρ αὐτοῦ καὶ ἡ ἀδελφὴ τῆς μητρὸς αὐτοῦ, Μαρία ἡ τοῦ Κλωπᾶ καὶ Μαρία ἡ Μαγδαληνή, "So the soldiers did this. But standing by the cross of Jesus were his mother, and his mother's sister, Mary the wife of Clopas, and Mary Magdalene" (v. 25).

Grammatically speaking, we have the comparison between the new narrative unit with δὲ, "now" (v. 25), with the previous narrative unit, which has in it μὲν, "indeed" (v. 24).[145] This contrast μὲν...δὲ helps to create a demarcation between the two narrative units. This means that v. 24 has ended the former narrative unit, and v. 25 begins a new one.[146] This new narrative unit continues until v. 27. Then, v. 28 begins a new narrative unit. V. 27 brings this narrative unit to a conclusion, and v. 28 begins a new one. The new Narrative unit is being introduced with

---

[144] Moloney holds that v. 24 ends the unit on "the decision not to tear apart the seamless garment" (19,23-24). Moloney treats 19, 25-27 as a textual unit with a focus on the topic of "the mother of Jesus and the beloved Disciple" (19, 25-27). See F. J. Moloney., "John", *The Paulist Biblical Commentary* (eds. J. E.A. Chiu—J. Clifford., et al) (New York—Mahwah 2018)1172.

[145] This is probably why Keener states that "on a literary level, Jesus' women supporters form a contrast to the soldiers just described (note the μὲν...δὲ construction in 19, 24-25);but their presence is historically likely as well as theologically suggestive (cf. Mark 15, 40-41)." Keener., *Gospel of John*, 1141. According to Barrett, it is possible that the soldiers might have allowed the women disciples of Jesus to remain among the "bystanders "there. See Barrett., *John*, 551.

[146] According to Bultmann as quoted in Tolmie, v.25 was used as a transition to v.26 because the interest of the evangelist was on the mother of Jesus. Cf. D. F. Tolmie., "The women by the Cross", 621. Also, worth noting is the fact that "the majority detect a contrast between the group of four women and the four soldiers who crucified Jesus" M. W. G. Stibbe., *John* (Sheffield 1993)194; H. Thyen., *Das Johannesevangelium* (HNT 6; Tübingen,2005) 737; G. R. Beasley-Murray, *John* (WBC 36; Waco, TX 1987)348.

the help of Μετὰ τοῦτο, "after this" in v. 28 stating Μετὰ τοῦτο εἰδὼς ὁ Ἰησοῦς ὅτι ἤδη πάντα τετέλεσται, ἵνα τελειωθῇ ἡ γραφή, λέγει· διψῶ, "After this Jesus, knowing that all was now finished, said (to fulfill the Scripture), "I thirst." So, a new narrative unit is being introduced in contrast with the prior narrative unit. The comparison is between the new narrative unit with δὲ, "now" (v. 25) with the previous narrative unit which has in it μὲν, "indeed" (v. 24). This contrast μὲν ... δὲ helps to create a demarcation between the two narrative units. This means that v. 24 has ended the former narrative unit, and v. 25 begins a new one, which continues until it ends at v. 27. Then, v. 28 begins another new narrative unit.

Thematically, we grasp that John 19, 17-30 has a larger theme: "the crucifixion and death of Jesus." Nevertheless, we can break it into smaller themes according to the narrative units for better clarity. Hence, the crucifixion of Jesus occurs in John 19, 17-24, which is a narrative unit prior to the narrative unit I am dealing with here, that is, 19, 25-27, with the theme of "at the foot of the cross," which in a sense reveals to us the place where this event is taking place. After our narrative unit comes a new one, beginning with v. 28 and ending with v. 30, with the theme of the death of Jesus.

2.1.3 An issue of Exegetical Interpretation (John 19, 25)

An issue of exegetical interpretation arises here in John 19, 25 with a focus on the number of women present at the scene of the cross of Jesus. The issue is whether there were 2 or 3 or 4 women at the cross of Jesus. The scholars disagree on the number of women, which has been pointed out in v. 25. Consequently, the interpretation of this verse Εἱστήκεισαν δὲ παρὰ τῷ σταυρῷ τοῦ Ἰησοῦ ἡ μήτηρ αὐτοῦ καὶ ἡ ἀδελφὴ τῆς μητρὸς αὐτοῦ, Μαρία ἡ τοῦ Κλωπᾶ καὶ Μαρία ἡ Μαγδαληνή (19, 25) has taken three different dimensions leading to the suggestions distinguishing two, three and four women being present at the site of the cross of Jesus.[147] Each of these is examined below.

2.1.3.1 Two women

According to this view of interpretation of Εἱστήκεισαν δὲ παρὰ τῷ σταυρῷ τοῦ Ἰησοῦ ἡ μήτηρ αὐτοῦ καὶ ἡ ἀδελφὴ τῆς μητρὸς αὐτοῦ, Μαρία ἡ τοῦ Κλωπᾶ καὶ Μαρία ἡ Μαγδαληνή (19, 25). The scholars who hold this view think that this verse refers only to two women, namely, the mother of Jesus and her sister. They are the same two women again appearing in the following clause with the names "Mary of Clopas" and "Mary Magdalene." Scholars typically reject this view because it may not be tenable that Mary, the mother of Jesus, would be called Mary of Clopas. Moreover, if we accept that Mary Magdalene was the sister of the mother of Jesus, then it would mean that their parents gave the same name, "Mary," to two of their daughters. This may not be the case. Further, since the mother of Jesus is not named in the gospel of John, it may mean that the objection in question may lose its force. This interpretation referring to two women is not popular among contemporary scholars.[148] Since this first one raises more problems, let us try to see what the other view suggesting three women has to say.

2.1.3.2 Three women

The Greek text Εἱστήκεισαν δὲ παρὰ τῷ σταυρῷ τοῦ Ἰησοῦ ἡ μήτηρ αὐτοῦ καὶ ἡ ἀδελφὴ τῆς μητρὸς αὐτοῦ, Μαρία ἡ τοῦ Κλωπᾶ καὶ Μαρία ἡ Μαγδαληνή (19, 25) is translated to distinguish only three women,

---

[147] Cf. Tolmie., *The Women by the Cross*, 624.

[148] See J. Blinzler., *Die Brüder und Schwester Jesu* (SBS 21; Stuttgart 1967)111, cites examples of some few scholars who supported this position of interpretation. These were scholars such as M. Schwalb, H. J. Holtzmann and G. M. de la Garenne.

namely, the mother of Jesus, the sister of the mother of Jesus who is being identified to be "Mary of Clopas" and finally Mary Magdalene.[149] This view again carries forward the problem of two sisters from the same parents having the same name, "Mary." For this reason, many scholars reject this interpretation as well. If we decide to interpret ἀδελφὴ in "a different way," like "sister – in – law" to substitute "sister," then we can overcome this objection based on the same name for two sisters. This kind of interpretation was proposed by Richard Bauckham in the study of the New Testament concerning "Mary of Clopas."[150] Here, we notice that the view which states that three women were present at the cross of Jesus leaves us with a challenge.

2.1.3.3 Four women

Some other scholars maintain that four women were mentioned in v. 25. Therefore, in translating Εἱστήκεισαν δὲ παρὰ τῷ σταυρῷ τοῦ Ἰησοῦ ἡ μήτηρ αὐτοῦ καὶ ἡ ἀδελφὴ τῆς μητρὸς αὐτοῦ, Μαρία ἡ τοῦ Κλωπᾶ καὶ Μαρία ἡ Μαγδαληνή (19, 25) four women may distinguished. Two of these women are identified by their relationship with Jesus, namely, the mother of Jesus and the sister to the mother of Jesus. Then, the remaining

---

[149] Wahlde supports this view of three women present at the foot of the cross of Jesus. He explains that in vv.25-27 among those who were standing around the foot of the cross were four disciples of Jesus. Three were women and one man. According to him, the three women were the mother of Jesus, Mary the wife of Clopas, and Mary from Magdala. Clopas was the brother of Joseph, who was the father of Jesus. Cf. Cf. U. C. von Wahlde, "John", *The Jerome Biblical Commentary for the Twenty-First Century* (eds. J. J. Collins., et al) (London — New York ³2022)1437.

[150] Cf. R. Bauckham., *Gospel Women*. Studies of the Named Women in the Gospels (Grand Rapids 2002) 203-223. See also, H. C. Waetjen., *The Gospel of the Beloved Disciple*. A Work in Two Editions (New York 2005) 397; T. K. Seim., "Roles of Women in the Gospel of John," *Aspects on the Johannine Literature: Papers Presented at a Conference of Scandinavian New Testament Exegetes at Uppsala, June 16-19,1986* (eds. L. Hartman - B. Olsson) (Stockholm 1987) 57-58.

two women are simply called Mary of Clopas and Mary Magdalene.[151] Indeed, in describing the configuration of the family of Jesus, Dauer affirms that there were four women present "by Jesus in the hour of his rejection."[152] Thereby supporting the view that there were four women just as Tolmie did.[153]

2.1.4 Text and Translation of John 19, 25-27[154]

2.1.4.1 Text : John 19, 25-27

25 Εἱστήκεισαν δὲ παρὰ τῷ σταυρῷ τοῦ Ἰησοῦ ἡ μήτηρ αὐτοῦ καὶ ἡ ἀδελφὴ τῆς μητρὸς αὐτοῦ, Μαρία ἡ τοῦ Κλωπᾶ καὶ ˥Μαρία ἡ Μαγδαληνή.

26 Ἰησοῦς οὖν ἰδὼν τὴν μητέρα καὶ τὸν μαθητὴν παρεστῶτα ὃν ἠγάπα, λέγει τῇ μητρί· γύναι, ἴδε ὁ υἱός σου.

27 εἶτα λέγει τῷ μαθητῇ· ἴδε ἡ μήτηρ σου. καὶ ἀπ' ἐκείνης τῆς ὥρας ἔλαβεν ὁ μαθητὴς αὐτὴν εἰς τὰ ἴδια.

2.1.4.2 Translation of John 19,25-27

v.25 So the soldiers did this. But standing by the cross of Jesus were his mother and his mother's sister, Mary, the wife of Clopas and Mary Magdalene.

---

[151] It is worth noting that, among these women being talked about, the mother of Jesus and her sister are not named in the text. The mother of Jesus was an honorary tittle given to her and was being used to emphasize her role which she fulfils in the Gospel. However, for her sister, it is suggested that may be this was the manner through which people knew her in "early Christianity or that her name was not preserved in the tradition." R. E. Brown, *The Death of the Messiah* (New York 1994) I, 1015.

[152] A. Dauer., *Die Passionsgeschichte in Johannesevangelium. Eine traditionsgeschichtliche und theologische Untersuchung zu Joh 18,1-19,30* (SANT 30; München 1972) 316-318.

[153] Like many Johannine scholars, Tolmie agree that there were four women at the foot of the cross. Cf. Tolmie., *The Women by the Cross*, 624. I personally find this view much vivid, so I support it.

[154] Unless otherwise explicitly stated, the translation of texts will be from The Holy Bible, *Revised Standard Version, Second Catholic Edition* (San Francisco, 1965) 97.

v.26 When Jesus saw his mother and the disciple whom he loved standing near, he said to his mother, "Woman, behold, your son!"

v.27 Then he said to the disciple, "behold, your mother!" And from that hour the disciple took her to his own home.

2.2 Narrative Structure and Analysis: Plot of John 19, 25-27

This narrative unit 19, 25-27 may be divided into four subunits to make a narrative structure with initial situation (19, 25), complication (19, 26a), Transformative action (vv. 26b-27a), resolution and final Situation (27b). Here below is the analysis of the text according to its narrative structural subunits.

2.2.1 Initial situation (John 19, 25)

In this initial situation, we see the new characters being introduced, standing by the side of the cross of Jesus. Εἰστήκεισαν δὲ παρὰ τῷ σταυρῷ τοῦ Ἰησοῦ ἡ μήτηρ αὐτοῦ καὶ ἡ ἀδελφὴ τῆς μητρὸς αὐτοῦ, Μαρία ἡ τοῦ Κλωπᾶ καὶ Μαρία ἡ Μαγδαληνή, "So the soldiers did this. But standing by the cross of Jesus were his mother, and his mother's sister, Mary the wife of Clopas, and Mary Magdalene" (John 19, 25)[155]. The text reveal that there was a group of people standing by the cross of Jesus comprising of "his mother, his mother's sister, Mary the wife of Clopas, and Mary Magdalene" (John 19, 25). Here we see the introduction and establishment of a group of persons who would later form part of the 'the new family' of Jesus."[156]

---

[155] According to Senior "that cold and Brutal ritual of the Roman soldiers sets up a sharp contrast with the next scene where the reader learns of the faithful presence of the women and the Beloved Disciple at the cross and sees the way Jesus himself will care for what belongs to him (John 19, 25b-27)" D. Senior., *The Passion of Jesus in the Gospel of John* (Collegeville —Minnesota, 1991)107.

[156] J. Zumstein., "The Mother of Jesus and the Beloved Disciple: How a New Family is Established under the Cross", 641; Cf. R. A. Culpepper., *Anatomy of the Fourth Gospel. A Study in Literary Design*, 99-148.

2.2.2 Complication (John 19, 26a)

Ἰησοῦς οὖν ἰδὼν τὴν μητέρα καὶ τὸν μαθητὴν παρεστῶτα ὃν ἠγάπα, "when Jesus saw his mother and the disciple whom he loved standing near" (John 19, 26a). The complication occurs here in John 19, 26a as we are given a surprise because of the presence of the beloved disciple.[157] This text brings to the reader τὸν μαθητὴν παρεστῶτα ὃν ἠγάπα, "the disciple whom he loved." Jesus saw the beloved disciple also standing near his cross. It is quite a surprise because, in the initial situation of the narrative unit, we did not see the beloved disciple being introduced, but now he is present.

This beloved disciple appears in the Gospel of John as "the one whom Jesus loved" (John 13, 23-26; 19, 26-27; 20, 2-10; 21, 7. 20-23) and "as an unnamed disciple" (John 1, 35-40; 18, 15-16). He is a "subject of the narrative asides in John 19, 35; 21,24),"[158] In John 19, 25-27, he is presented as an obedient and faithful disciple of Jesus, the only male disciple at the foot of the cross of Jesus. The disciple to whom Jesus gave his mother and this act deepens his already existing close relationship with Jesus even more. His close relationship with Jesus is enhanced and confirmed by the fact that he is the one to whom Jesus handed over his mother (cf. John 19, 25-27). This disciple is "the ideal disciple, a

---

[157] Cf. D. Senior., *The Passion of Jesus in the Gospel of John* (Collegeville—Minnesota, 1991) 108, affirms that the Gospel of John mentions the presence of the mother of Jesus and the beloved disciple meanwhile other gospels never mentions. D. Senior., *The Passion of Jesus in the Gospel of John*,108.

[158] R. Bauckham., *The Testimony of the Beloved Disciple. Narrative, History, and Theology in the Gospel of John* (Grand Rapids 2007) 73-91. However, Bennema "argues that he is the ideal eyewitness", see Bennema., *Encountering Jesus,* 171-182.

paradigm of discipleship."[159] He is "the ideal witness and ideal author."[160] This disciple appears here with a "role as the voice of this point of view... represents the ideal point of view[161] of the narrative."[162] This is probably why Lincoln thinks that "among the male disciples, the beloved Disciple represents this ideal perspective." [163] Therefore, He is a disciple with a special relationship, a "closest communion" with Jesus.[164] No wonder Jesus gave him his mother. Bauckham notes that the beloved disciple followed devotedly, remained with Jesus, and witnessed the "key event of the Gospel: Jesus' glorification on the cross."[165] His character is static.[166] Nevertheless, Jesus gave him authority over the new family he created on the cross and asked him to "compensate" for his own "inevitable absence"

---

[159] Cf. C. Koester., *Symbolism in the Fourth Gospel*. Meaning, Mystery, Community (Minneapolis, ²2003) 242; R. F. Collins., "The Representative figures of the Fourth Gospel," *DRev* 94 (1976) 132; R. A. Culpepper., *Anatomy of the Fourth Gospel*. A Study in Literary Design (Philadelphia 1983) 121-123; W. S. Kurz., "The Beloved Disciple and Implied Readers," *BTB* 19 (1989)100-107.

[160] J. L. Ressseguie., "The Beloved Disciple: The Ideal point of View", *Characters Studies in the Fourth Gospel* (eds. S. A. Hunt., — D.F. Tolmie., — R. Zimmermann) (Tübingen 2013) 537. Bauckham argues that identifying the beloved disciple as the model of discipleship creates a difficulty. He argues that "although the disciple may function as a paradigm of discipleship in the narrative   as do other disciples such as Nathanael and Mary Magdalene — it is misleading to view him as the disciple *par excellence*", R. Bauckham., *The Testimony of the beloved disciple*, 82-85.

[161] Abrams and Resseguie holds that, point of view "signifies the way a story gets told," M. H. Abrams., *A Glossary of Literary Terms* (Fort Worth ⁷1999) s.v. "point of view"; J. L. Ressseguie., *Narrative Criticism of the New Testament*, 167.

[162] Ressseguie., "The Beloved Disciple: The Ideal point of View", 537.

[163] A. T. Lincoln., "The Beloved Disciple as Eyewitness and the Fourth Gospel as Witness," *JSNT* 85 (2002) 10.

[164] J. L. Ressseguie., "The Beloved Disciple: The Ideal point of View", 539.

[165] Bauckham., *Testimony*, 82-87.

[166] He is presented as a static character despite the fact that he has a very significant role in "voicing the ideal point of view of the Gospel. He does not "stumble over" the words of Jesus nor misinterpret his action. See J. L. Ressseguie., "The Beloved Disciple: The Ideal point of View", 549.

as a son to his mother.[167] The beloved disciple, on his part, remained "a trustworthy witness.

John 19, 25 "adds another follower, the beloved disciple."[168] As the narrative develops further, the central focus shall be on the two: the mother of Jesus and the beloved disciple. Interestingly, both of them remained unnamed. They are simply called ἡ μήτηρ αὐτοῦ, "his mother" (v. 26a), and ὁ μαθητὴς ὃν ἠγάπα, "the disciple whom he loved" (v. 26a) without giving them specific names to "clarify their relationships to Jesus. In each case, the designations are characteristic of closeness, markers of intimacy."[169] This makes a lot of sense to me and I may view the mother of Jesus and the beloved disciple as people who had intimate relationship with Jesus.

2.2.3 Transformative action (John 19, 26b-27a)

26b λέγει τῇ μητρί· γύναι, ἴδε ὁ υἱός σου, "he said to his mother, "Woman, behold, your son!" 27a εἶτα λέγει τῷ μαθητῇ· ἴδε ἡ μήτηρ σου, "then he said to the disciple, "Behold, your mother!".[170] In his transformative action (19, 26a-27a), Jesus addressed his mother, and the

---

[167] J. Zumstein., "The Mother of Jesus and the Beloved Disciple: How a New Family is Established under the Cross", *Character Studies in the Fourth Gospel* (eds. S. A. Hunt., — D.F. Tolmie., — R. Zimmermann) (Tübingen 2013) 644.

[168] J. Zumstein., "The Mother of Jesus and the Beloved Disciple: How a New Family is Established under the Cross", 641.

[169] J. Zumstein., "The Mother of Jesus and the Beloved Disciple: How a New Family is Established under the Cross", 641-642.

[170] Senior holds that in this way Jesus has entrusted his mother to the care of the disciple whom he loved. He showed a gesture filled with grace. This demonstrates that he is a faithful son. D. Senior., *The Passion of Jesus in the Gospel of John* (Collegeville 1991)108.

beloved disciple present near his cross, as seen in the text above.[171] Here, the narrator portrays Jesus as the only one speaking. The mother of Jesus and the beloved disciple listened in silence.[172] Therefore, Jesus wisely spoke to his mother and the disciple he loved while they remained "fully passive and silent."[173] Just like in other parts of the Gospel of John, the mother of Jesus is not named. She is not named in order to "emphasize her dispossession as his mother. Initially, she is introduced as 'his mother'(John 19, 25)...more generally as "mother" (John 19, 26a two times). Jesus addresses Mary as a 'woman,' which places distance between himself and his mother."[174]

---

[171] Moloney notes that Jesus was lifted up on the cross. While up there he spoke to the woman who was the first character to commit herself in unconditional way to his word (cf. 2, 3-5). He commanded her to see and to accept the beloved disciple as her own son. He then turned to the Beloved disciple and gave him a command to see his mother ("the mother of Jesus") and to accept her also as his mother. The two obeyed these words of Jesus without any query. This is why the narrator stated that "from that hour the disciple took her into his own home"(John 19, 27). Cf. Moloney., "John", 1172.

[172] The mother of Jesus and the beloved disciple never spoke. Only Jesus spoke to both of them. He spoke to each of them at a time. He said to his mother "woman, here is your son." This phrase might be considered as he was referring to himself. However, the words that he told the disciple whom he loved makes us think he was giving the disciple whom he loved to his mother as a son to her. In the same manner he did inform this disciple whom he loved that Mary is now his mother. Consequently, with these words, the death of Jesus on the cross created a new family. See B. Lindars., *John.* New Testament Guides (Sheffield 1990) 578-580; C. R. Koester., *Symbolism in the Fourth Gospel. Meaning, Mystery, Community* (Minneapolis,1995) 243.

[173] J. Zumstein., "The Mother of Jesus and the Beloved Disciple: How a New Family is Established under the Cross", 642. Infact, Schürmann argues that "the scene at the foot of the cross offers virtually nothing which allows the role and the meaning of the mother to be explained" H. Schürmann., "Jesu letzte Weisung. Jo 19, 26-27a.", *Ders., Ursprung und Gestalt. Erörterungen und Beinnungen zum Neuen Testament. Spricht von einem.* Rätselwort (1970) 20-22.

[174] Cf. D. R. Beck., *The Discipleship Paradigm.* Readers and Anonymous Characters in the Fourth Gospel (Bis 27; Leiden 1997) 55.

The transformative action is done by Jesus in verses 26b - 27a.[175] They only acted by bringing to a realization and fulfillment of all that Jesus said to them from the cross. In line with the Jewish family law, Jesus gave his mother to the beloved disciple so that he could protect her after he was gone. The beloved disciple would take over Jesus's responsibility of caring for his mother. He stands in the place of Jesus in taking care of her.[176] However, Dauer makes a point that the mother of Jesus was not given the responsibility of taking care of the disciple whom Jesus loved.[177] According to Zumstein, the presence of the beloved disciple at the cross should be interpreted as "the presence of witness."[178]

Through the same words of Jesus on the cross, the mother of Jesus and the beloved disciple became the symbols of the *Familia Dei*, "the family of God," that Jesus created through his wise words. It follows that at the cross, Jesus formed *Familia Dei*, "the family of God." The word "family" is "the semantic field, "which in our context here refers to the "pair of mother and son," which focuses on establishing "a new relationship within this family." At the time of the death of Jesus, he set a base for this new family

---

[175] Since a widow was vulnerable, some think that Jesus did this to take care of his mother after his death. He therefore acted in a just manner and with care towards his mother. See D. Senior., *The passion of Jesus according to John*, 109. Wahlde adds that Jesus addressed his mother from the cross proclaiming that from that very moment on his disciple was to be her son and he also spoke to the beloved disciple proclaiming to him that his mother would now be the mother of the beloved disciple as well. Cf. U. C. von Wahlde., "John", 1437.

[176] J. Zumstein., "The Mother of Jesus and the Beloved Disciple: How a New Family is Established under the Cross", 642.

[177] Dauer., *Passionsgeschichte*, 323—326. This is a Mariological interpretation. There was no expectation either of a "relationship of mutual partnership. Only the Beloved Disciple is entrusted with a mission. He must take the Mother 'into his home'", J. Zumstein., "The Mother of Jesus and the Beloved Disciple: How a New Family is Established under the Cross", 642.

[178] J. Zumstein., "The Mother of Jesus and the Beloved Disciple: How a New Family is Established under the Cross", 643.

that would exist after his death. He established the "post-Easter family." Subsequently, "both the characters of the Mother of Jesus and the beloved disciple are transformed into one collective character. From now on, they constitute and exemplify the core substance of the *Familia Dei*."[179] Jesus addressed his mother and the beloved disciple, thereby creating a new family. In this way, he did perform a transformative action (John 19, 26b-27a).

2.2.4 Resolution and Final Situation (John 19, 27b)

In John 19, 27b καὶ ἀπ' ἐκείνης τῆς ὥρας ἔλαβεν ὁ μαθητὴς αὐτὴν εἰς τὰ ἴδια, "and from that hour the disciple took her to his own home" In this verse, we have a resolution and the final situation of the narrative unit. In the previous subunit of the transformative action, the mother of Jesus and the beloved disciple remained silent while listening to the words of Jesus. In this subunit of the resolution and final situation, they now demonstrate by their action that they understood and accepted the words that Jesus spoke to them. The beloved disciple and the mother of Jesus accepted the will of Jesus. The disciple whom Jesus loved received the mother of Jesus in his own home as his own mother.

2.3 Key Elements in John 19, 25-27

2.3.1 The women by the cross (John 19, 25)

Four women are introduced in this narrative pericope (19, 25). They were present by the cross of Jesus. They are the mother of Jesus, the sister

---

[179] Cf. P. Ricoeur., *De L'interprétation*. Essais sur Freud (L'ordre Philosophique, Paris1965) 20-27; J. Zumstein., "The Mother of Jesus and the Beloved Disciple: How a New *Family is Established under the Cross*", 642.

of the mother of Jesus, Mary, the wife of Clopas and Mary Magdalene[180]. These women are composed of two major characters and two minor characters. The two minor characters are the sister of the mother of Jesus and Mary, the wife of Clopas. The two major characters are the mother of Jesus and Mary Magdalene. They play very important roles in this narrative. The mother of Jesus was introduced earlier in the narrative text of 2, 1-12, while Mary Magdalene is introduced at the foot of the cross for the first time. Mary Magdalene will play a very important role later.[181]

These two women, who are the major characters, "meet" here in this narrative cosmos.[182] Both of these two major characters were called γύναι, "woman" by Jesus in their lifetime. Subsequently, 19, 25-27 is a scene where these two major characters meet. The use of μὲν ... δὲ suggests that there is a contrast between "the group" of these women and that of the soldiers (v. 25). The women were standing there all along. The use of the pluperfect verb Εἱστήκεισαν, "had been standing" (v. 25) [183] referring to the action of these women, may indicate that they had been standing there right from when the

---

[180] Mary Magdalene was the third woman from the hometown of Magdala. The word "Migdal," means "tower". Subsequently, this name could have been given her to demonstrate that she was the tower of strength and fidelity. This is the woman who will be the first to see the Lord Jesus after his resurrection(20:14). Cf. U. C. von Wahlde., "John", 1437.

[181] Cf. Tolmie., *The Women by the Cross,"* 621.

[182] This fact of their meeting has been pointed out by Judith Lieu. See J.M. Lieu., "The *Mother of the Son in the Fourth Gospel," JBL* 117/1(1998) 68.

[183] The usage of pluperfect verb is usually meant to expose an event and to provide a "background information". In this context of 19, 25, the verb Εἱστήκεισαν (pluperfect, indicative, active, 3rd plural of ἵστημι) is meant to expose an event. See R. E. Brown., *Death of the Messiah,*1013; J. Frey., *Die Johanneische Eschatologie II.* Das johanneische Zeitverständnis (WUNT 110; Tübingen 1998)*115-116.*

crucifixion process started. The words "were standing there" could be seen as "an analepsis."[184]

The soldiers acted "in the most horrific" manner to Jesus, but these women supported Jesus. This support is not stated explicitly in the text, but we can deduce it since they are standing there by the cross of Jesus. The use of ἵστημι in other parts of the gospel of John, such as John 1, 35; 3, 29 "where John the Baptist 'stands' as a witness could possibly be cited in support of the above "interpretation."[185] Carson is quoted in Tolmie to confirm that these women waited in "faithful devotion to the one whose death they can still only understand as tragedy."[186]

The presence of these women followers of Jesus at the cross is important to note. Their presence contrasts the absence of the disciples, whose presence should have been there but was absent; they deserted Jesus except for the disciple whom Jesus loved. When we contrast the women to the disciples, one can say these women were indeed "the faithful few."[187]

The women did abide with Jesus. Indeed, the use of the preposition παρὰ in 19, 25 with the verb "standing" implies the idea of "abiding." Further, contrasting this group of four women with the men, we find

---

[184] This means the action is narrated "after" the action has occurred already but not at the very moment it occurred. For more details on how to do the analysis of temporal relations in a narrative text, see D. F. Tolmie., *Narratology and Biblical Narratives. A Practical Guide* (San Francisco 1999) 87-103.

[185] Tolmie., "The Women by the Cross",622.

[186] Tolmie., "The Women by the Cross",623.

[187] F. D. Brunner., *The Gospel of John. A Commentary* (Grand Rapids 2012)1107. These women followed Jesus all through to the very end and even remained with him there. Cf. Tolmie., "The Women by the Cross",623.

that the women followed and supported Jesus more. The men, of course, deserted him except for the disciple Jesus loved.[188]

The women never resisted the initiatives of Jesus; they never failed to believe, neither did they desert Jesus. They also never betrayed him. The male gender is seen to have been "vain" (13, 37); "hypocritical" (12, 4-6); "fickle" (13, 38; 16, 31-32); "deliberately unbelieving" (9, 24-41; 20, 24-25) or "thoroughly evil" (13, 2. 27-30)."[189] Viewing these women as "subjects," we note that they followed Jesus all the way to the cross and continued to remain there, standing and supporting him. Viewing these women from the perspective of being "objects" to whom an action is "being done," these four women found themselves at the foot of the cross of Jesus. This is because Jesus drew them to himself. [190]

Thus far, one may deduce that these women followers of Jesus were so important as they followed him faithfully and supported him at his lowest moment of life. The mother of Jesus is one of them. All the roles played by these women as a group apply to each of them individually.

---

[188] S. M. Schneiders., "Women in the Fourth Gospel," *The Gospel of John as Literature. An Anthology of Twentieth-Century Perspectives* (M. W. G. STIBBE) (NTTS 17; Leiden 1993)129; See also C. M. Conway., *Men and Women in the Fourth Gospel. Gender and Johannine Characterization* (SBLDS 167; Atlanta,1999) 205.

[189] Tolmie, "The Women by the Cross", 623.

[190] Cf. Brown., *Death of the Messiah*, 1019. This is what Jesus "predicted" saying "when I am lifted up from the earth, I will draw all to myself" (John 12, 32). These women were the first people to be drawn by Jesus to himself at the time when he was being lifted up on the cross. In John 19, 26-27 they are also members of the family of Jesus. The first two in the list of them (that is, the mother of Jesus and her sister) are members of the biological family of Jesus hence emphasizing the idea of family. This idea of family is later interpreted in a larger sense in John 19, 26-27 to mean a "new spiritual family" which was created by Jesus at the foot of the cross. Since the mother of Jesus is mentioned first in the list of these women, it may point to the level of importance of her role in the gospel of John. Cf. J. Hartenstein., *Charakterisierung im Dialog.* Maria Magdalena, Petrus, Thomas und die Mutter Jesu im Johannesevangelium im Kontext anderer frühchristlicher Darstellungen (NTOA/SUNT 64; Göttingen 2007)274.

This means, from the roles played as a group, the mother of Jesus, being one of the members of this group, can be named as one who played a role in the same manner as other members. Any role played by the group collectively can also be said of her as her own proper role at the foot of the cross. She was present, followed Jesus till the end of his life, accompanied him, supported him, listened to him, and stood by his cross in support of her son. She allowed herself to be drawn by Jesus to the cross when he was being lifted up on it.

2.3.2 γύναι, "woman" (John 19, 26a)[191]

Jesus said to his mother, "Woman, behold, your son!" (John 19, 26). He addressed his mother with the title γύναι, "woman" (John 19, 26) as he had done before in John 2, 4; 4, 21; 8, 10; 20, 13.15. This scene of John 19, 25-27 is a meeting point between two women whom Jesus used this title to call. Jesus called his mother "woman" and later in his resurrection power called Mary Magdalene "woman" as well.[192] According to Barosse, some people link the title γύναι, "woman" of the mother of Jesus, "with a new Eve."[193]

2.3.3 ἀπ' ἐκείνης τῆς ὥρας "from that hour" (John 19, 27)

The narrator stated that καὶ ἀπ' ἐκείνης τῆς ὥρας ἔλαβεν ὁ μαθητὴς αὐτὴν εἰς τὰ ἴδια, "and from that hour the disciple took her to his own home" (John 19, 27b). At Cana of Galilee, Jesus himself talked about the

---

[191] According to Senior, "Jesus does not address Mary as "Mother" but as "woman"— reminiscent of the same address used of her in the Cana Story (John 2, 4)." D. Senior., *The Passion of Jesus in the Gospel of John*, 109. Manelli, noted that Jesus called his mother "woman" and that this is the same term that he had used at Cana in John 2:4. S. M. Manelli., *Mariologia Biblica*, 400.

[192] Cf. Tolmie., *The Women by the Cross*, 621.

[193] T. Barosse., "The Seven Days of the New Creation in St. John's Gospel", *CBQ* 21 (1959) 516.

"hour," saying to his mother τί ἐμοὶ καὶ σοί, γύναι; οὔπω ἥκει ἡ ὥρα μου, "what to me and to you woman, my hour is not yet come" (John 2, 4)[194]. The first mention of the "hour" in John 2, 4 was meant to say that the time of Jesus had not yet arrived, for he was still at the beginning of his public life. The narrator mentioned the word "hour" again here at the foot of the cross to mark out the hour or the time upon which she was taken as mother by the disciple whom Jesus loved. After the marriage feast at Cana of Galilee, she departed with her son Jesus to Capernaum, but at this "hour," she now departs with her "new son," the beloved disciple (John 19, 27b). The time marks this drastic change in her life and the life of the disciple whom Jesus loved.

Zumstein holds that when Jesus talked about "hour" (John 2, 4) at the feast of the wedding at Cana of Galilee, he referred beyond "the sign" to a "decisive hour" of the future well mentioned by the narrator as ἀπ' ἐκείνης τῆς ὥρας, "from that hour" (John 19, 27). This decisive hour would open "the door to the Post-Easter future."[195] In the "Book of Signs," the hour of Jesus had not yet come (John 2, 4; 7, 30; 8, 20). Also, at the end of the Book of Signs, the theme of glorification starts (John 12, 23) after the triumphal entry of Jesus into Jerusalem. Some of these themes are found in John 11, 45-54; 12, 1-11. The salvation to be brought about by Jesus will be accomplished through the death and resurrection of Jesus himself. In this light, the

---

[194] Murray maintains that this "hour" refers to the "Messianic task of Jesus". G. R. Beasley-Murray., *John* (WBC 36) (Waco, TX ²1999) 32. We must be aware that "it was Jesus' answer to his mother's request, close to the opening of the Gospel narrative, that began Jesus' journey toward his" hour"(John 2, 4); now he makes final preparations for his mother after his departure (John 19, 26-27)...the closing passage completes the issue introduced in the earlier one; Jesus can ultimately care for his mother's needs only in his 'hour'..." Keener., *The Gospel of John. A Commentary*, 1143.

[195] J. Zumstein., "The Mother of Jesus and the Beloved Disciple: How a New Family is Established under the Cross", 644.

"hour" ought to be interpreted to mean the entire time of the passion of Jesus.[196] According to Nicholson, as quoted in Donald Senior, this "hour" being referred to is to be taken to be referring to the exaltation of Jesus by God.[197]

There is a play on two possible meanings for the translation of the Greek expression ἀπ᾽ ἐκείνης τῆς ὥρας, "from that hour" (John 19, 27). This expression may have a temporal meaning "from that particular time." Yet, the theological and dramatic importance of "the hour of Jesus" may give the Greek preposition ἀπό, followed by the genitive case ὥρας, a causative meaning, "because of that hour." This means that as a consequence of the lifting up of Jesus on the cross, his "hour," his mother, and the beloved disciple became one.[198]

2.4 Setting of John 19, 25 - 27

The text itself notes that the setting of this pericope is παρὰ τῷ σταυρῷ τοῦ Ἰησοῦ, "by the cross of Jesus" (v. 25). Manelli states that Jesus was

---

[196] Infact, In the synoptic gospels, the "hour" refers to the messianic time, the hour of the passion. Jesus prayed in the garden that, if possible, that hour was taken from him (Mark 14, 35). During the time of his arrest, he said to his disciples: "... It is enough; the hour has come; the Son of man is betrayed into the hands of sinners"(Mark 14, 41). The life of Jesus is tuned towards the fulfillment of that hour. He even named it "my hour"(John 2, 4). This hour has come for the son of man to be glorified (John 12, 23).This hour for the first time is about glorification (see in John 13, 1; 17, 1). His hour is the hour when he reaches the peak of his love. The life of Jesus is a gift, and it is supreme expression of his love. This is demonstrated in the washing of the feet when he puts off his out garment and again puts it on (John 13, 4. 12). This glorification of Jesus has to happen by way of his death (John 12, 24).

[197] Cf. D. Senior., *The Passion of Jesus in the Gospel of John*, 34. This is well supported by Moloney when he stated that "the Cross is the hour of Jesus". F. J. Moloney., "John" 1172.

[198] F. J. Moloney., "John", 1172-1173.

crucified at Golgotha.[199] Scott adds that Jesus was crucified outside the city when the crowds came to celebrate the Passover.[200] According to Wahlde, Jesus was crucified a day before Passover.[201]

This is the setting where the "new family" of Jesus is introduced by the pericope.[202] It was in Jerusalem. The Galileans who were on pilgrimage in Jerusalem might have brought back a message to her about the death of Jesus and so asked her to go to Jerusalem to "claim his corpse" before she received the message about the resurrection of her son Jesus.[203] This may imply that Jerusalem was where he was crucified and died.

Jesus was crucified and later buried in a garden (John 19, 41; 20, 15). In this garden, there was a tomb that had not been used to bury anyone. This kind of tomb belonged to the upper-class families. It was made for a family to use for many generations. It served the purpose of burial for a longer duration of time. Jesus was crucified within a quarry.[204]

---

[199] Cf. S. M. Manelli., *Mariologia Biblica,* 400. Moloney confirms this as he holds that Jesus was crucified at Golgotha, the place of the skull (v.17b). He added that the Roman soldiers were involved in the crucifixion of Jesus. The soldiers divided the garments of Jesus into 4 parts but they casted lots for his seamless inner garment in order not to tear it asunder (vv.23-24).This is because the unity of something precious to Jesus had to be kept. He was crucified between two others. In the synoptic gospels these two were bandits(cf. Mark 15:27; Matt 27:38) or Criminals(cf. Luke 23:39-43) but we don't find these pieces of information in the narrative account of the Gospel of John. For John, Jesus is the central focus even if he is crucified with the two. The narrator stated, "they crucified him" (v. 18b). Jesus is the 'centerpiece of a triptych of crucified' persons. See F. J. Moloney., "John", 1172.

[200] Cf. J. M. C. Scott, "John", *Eerdmans Commentary on the Bible* (eds. J. D. G. Dunn—J. W. Rogerson) (Michigan — Cambridge, 2003) 1206.

[201] Cf. U. C. von Wahlde., "John", 1437.

[202] J. Zumstein., "The Mother of Jesus and the Beloved Disciple: How a New Family is Established under the Cross", 641.

[203] Cf. B. J. Malina., *The New Testament World.* Insights from Cultural Anthropology (Atlanta 1981) 99. However, she was in Jerusalem for the Passover(7, 10; Luke 2, 41-42).

[204] Cf. U. C. von Wahlde., "John", 1436.

Jesus was condemned, crucified, and died.[205] He carried his own cross[206] from the Praetorium via Gennath Gate into Golgotha, the "place of the skull," where he was crucified with two other people, one on either side of him. On a placard, Pilate wrote a charge against him: "Jesus of Nazareth, the King of the Jews."[207] Some bystanders resisted this and wanted it changed. They wanted it written, "Jesus claimed to be King of the Jews," but Pilate refused to change. He told them, "What I have written, I have written." This placard, without any intention, revealed the entire truth about Jesus.[208] Pilate wrote in Hebrew, Latin, and Greek (19, 20b), the languages of the cultured world of the Roman Empire.[209]

2.5 Intratextuality and Intertextuality

2.5.1 Intratextuality

There are intratextual connections within the passages in the gospel of John based on Jesus and his mother. The mother of Jesus appears in John 2, 1-12 and John 19, 25-27 and is mentioned in passing in John 6, 42. In John 2, 1-12; 19, 25 - 27, the term ἡ μήτηρ (τοῦ Ἰησοῦ) is used to refer to the mother of Jesus. Jesus speaks to his mother in a direct way using the vocative case γύναι (John 2, 4; 4, 21; 8, 10; 20, 13.15); the theme of "the hour" is used (John 2, 4; 19, 27b) and of course, Jesus and his mother relate in an intimate way as son and mother with trust.

---

[205] It should be note that, his crucifixion led to his death. His legs were supposed to be broken. Before his legs were broken, he was already dead. So, they never broke his legs. This is viewed as a fulfilment of Scripture. Cf. U. C. von Wahlde., "John", 1438.

[206] Cf. F. J. Moloney., "John", 1172.

[207] F. J. Moloney., "John", 1172.

[208] Cf. U. C. von Wahlde., "John", 1436.

[209] In this way, the kingship of Jesus was proclaimed in a universal manner allowing all who passed there to read (v.20a).The use of many languages in proclaiming the kingship of Jesus also indicated that Jesus is drawing all people to himself (cf. 10,16;11:49-52;12, 32). See F. J. Moloney., "John", 1172.

The beloved disciple appeared at the foot of the cross (John 19, 25-27), where Jesus told him, "Here is your mother". Then he took her into his own home right from that hour. The presence of the beloved disciple is also seen in key parts of the Gospel of John. For example, "at the beginning (John 1, 35-40); at the last supper (John 13, 23-26); at Peter's denial (John 18, 15-16); at the tomb (John 20, 2-10); 21, 7. 20-23. When the risen Lord Jesus appeared at the sea of Tiberias, he announced, "It is the Lord!" (21, 7). The beloved disciple is the one who saw "the significance of Jesus's death on the cross and steps into the narrative to remind the reader of the importance of this event" (19, 35).[210] Mary Magdalene is mentioned here at the cross (19, 25) and in 20, 1-2. 11-18.

2.5.2 Intertextuality

There is also intertextual connection between John 19, 25-27 and the synoptic gospels based on the mention of the women at the site of the crucifixion of Jesus. For example, in Luke 24, 10, women such as Mary Magdalene, Joanna and Mary the mother of James and other women with them are mentioned to have been at the tomb . Also, Luke 23, 49 mentions that there were women there who had followed Jesus from Galilee. Mark 15, 40-41 mentions Mary Magdalene, Mary, the mother of James the Younger and of Joses, and Salome (v.40) and many other women who had come with him to Jerusalem (v.41). Then Matthew 27, 56 refers to Mary Magdalene, Mary the mother of James and Joseph, and the mother of the sons of Zebedee. The mention of these women brings

---

[210] J. L. Ressseguie., "The Beloved Disciple: The Ideal point of View", 549.

about the intertextual relationship among these texts of the synoptic gospels and John 19, 25-27.[211]

2.6 The mother of Jesus and the beloved disciple at the foot of the cross (John 19, 25-27)

The "mother of Jesus"[212] appears for the second and the last time in John. She is at the foot of the cross of Jesus together with other disciples of Jesus, including the beloved disciple.[213] She accompanied Jesus even here at his low moments.[214] She remained quiet, silent without speech. Jesus is the only one who speaks. The narrator does not give us the point of view of

---

[211] Despite the fact that there are these intertextual links, we ought to note that there are some differences as well. For instance, in the synoptic gospels, each of them mentions women after the death of Jesus and they note that they stood at a distance, looking from a far (Luke 23, 49; Mark 15, 40; Matt 27, 55) while in John the women are standing near the cross and are actually present before Jesus dies. Cf. Brown., *The Death of the Messiah*, 1017. Jesus even talked to his mother (John 19, 26b). So, Only in John Jesus is said to have interacted with these people who are present there at the foot of his cross before his death(19, 26). Mary Magdalene is listed in John and the synoptics, but only John mentions the presence of the Mother of Jesus, the sister of the mother of Jesus, Mary the wife of Clopas, and the Beloved disciple (John 19, 25 27). Luke may allude to the presence of the disciples of Jesus when he notes that "all those who knew Jesus" were there including those women who had followed him from Galilee(cf. Luke 23, 49).Cf. D. Senior., *The Passion of Jesus in the Gospel of John,* 108.

[212] The term "the mother of Jesus was regarded as an honorary title...might have been used to underline the symbolic role that she fulfills in the Gospel." D. F. Tolmie., "The Women by the Cross", 620.

[213] It is said that "the presence of the mother of Jesus is not mentioned in the synoptic line of Tradition but is plausible and consistent with her reported presence in Jerusalem a short time later (Acts 1, 14)." Keener., *The Gospel of John. A Commentary,* vol 2,1143.

[214] This is confirmed even by Zumstein who holds that the mother of Jesus "had faithfully accompanied Jesus from Cana to the crucifixion". J. Zumstein., "The Mother of Jesus and the Beloved Disciple: How a New Family is Established under the Cross", 644-645.

the mother of Jesus but only that of Jesus. The mother of Jesus received the final filial care of her son at the foot of the cross. Jesus performed one last act of filial piety, ensuring she would be cared for well when he was finally gone (19, 26-27).

Zumstein noted that, at the end of the life of Jesus on earth, he left his mother under the care of the beloved disciple[215]. He did not give this responsibility to his brothers but to the disciple whom he loved. This act disassociated her from the brothers of Jesus as well. Ignace de la Potterie believes that the mother of Jesus took responsibility over the church, given to her to protect and intercede for her as a way of showing care for her.[216]

According to Zumstein, the mother of Jesus "functions as a textual signal which marks the beginning and the end of the public ministry of Jesus."[217] The mother of Jesus was naturally and spiritually connected to Jesus, her son. She also represents the collective faith of Israel.[218] We ought to note that, Just like the mother of the text of Rev 12, 1-3, the mother of Jesus occasionally stands for the new Eve and a mother "of the spiritual community of Israel."[219]

---

[215] Zumstein noted that at the foot of the cross of Jesus, the future of the mother of Jesus was taken care of by the disciple whom Jesus loved. He took her into his own home as his own mother and even gave her "protection and hospitality" required. J. Zumstein., "The Mother of Jesus and the Beloved Disciple: How a New Family is Established under the Cross", 644.

[216] Cf. I. de la Potterie., *La Passion de Jésus Selon L'évangile de Jean,* 144-165.

[217] J. Zumstein., "The Mother of Jesus and the Beloved Disciple: How a New Family is Established under the Cross", 644.

[218] Cf. J. Zumstein., "The Mother of Jesus and the Beloved Disciple: How a New Family is Established under the Cross", 644.

[219] Cf. E. C. Hoskyns., "Genesis I-III and St. John's Gospel." *JTS* 21/83 (1919) 211-213; P. F. Ellis., *The Genius of John.* A Composition-Critical Commentary on the Fourth Gospel (Collegeville 1984) 271. It is worth noting that, "the specific meaning in Rev 12 is clearer, but even there the Mariological reading is unclear unless one resorts to subsequent tradition." C. S. Keener., *Revelation.* NIV Application Commentary (Grand Rapids,2000) 313-314,325-327.

The mother of Jesus also learned a lesson. Discipleship must be the larger context in which her role as a mother is delimited and defined."[220] Jesus honored his mother by guarding against the shame that she could have gotten later after his death. This is why it is noted by Malina and Neyrey that "both Luke (Acts 1, 14) and John may uphold Jesus' honor by guarding the shame of Mary by locating her in a new family, an honorable household, the church."[221] Like other women at the cross, the mother of Jesus, supported him, listened to him, and later responded accordingly as directed by her son Jesus (John 19, 25-27).

The mother of Jesus, a model of faith, and the disciple whom Jesus loved are now one as the disciple accepted her as a mother (John 19, 27) and unconditionally accepted the word of Jesus. The new family that Jesus formed at the cross also included his mother. The expression "mother" in John 19, 25-27 occurs not less than five times, for example, in v. 25 (twice), v. 26 (twice), and v. 27. The use of the expression "mother of Jesus" earlier in John 2, 1-5 where she was to accept first the word of Jesus, now comes into play as she now becomes the mother of the Beloved disciple at the foot of the cross onwards (John 19, 25-27). The beloved disciple ought to look after the widowed mother of Jesus after the death of Jesus, and the mother of Jesus holds a maternal role in the new family established at the cross by Jesus himself.[222]

---

[220] B. Witherington., *Women in the Ministry of Jesus*. A Study of Jesus' Attitudes to Women and Their Roles as Reflected in His Earthly Life (SNTSMS 51; Cambridge 1984) 95.

[221] B. J. Malina., — J. H. Neyrey., "Honor and Shame in Luke-Acts: Pivotal Values of the Mediterranean World", *The Social World of Luke-Acts: Models for Interpretation* (ed. J. H. Neyrey) (Peabody 1991) 64.

[222] Cf. J. Moloney., "John", 1173.

2.7 Conclusion.

This second chapter was dedicated to the exegetical study of John 19, 25-27. The main focus of its discussion was on the mother of Jesus at the foot of the cross (John 19, 25-27). This chapter was introduced, then discussed the preliminary matters that included context of John 19, 25-27, delimitation of John 19, 25-27, an issue of exegetical interpretation in John 19, 25 (two women, three women, four women), and text and translation of John 19, 25-27. The chapter proceeded with the study of the narrative structure and analysis: plot of John 19, 25-27 (initial situation in John 19, 25; complication in John 19, 26a; transformative action in John 19, 26b-27a; and the resolution and final situation in John 19, 27b). We also discussed key elements in John 19, 25-27 by looking at the women by the cross (John 19, 25); γύναι, "woman" (John 19, 26a); and ἀπ' ἐκείνης τῆς ὥρας "from that hour" (John 19, 27). Furthermore, in this chapter we considered setting of John 19, 25 – 27, intratextual and Intertextual connections with other texts within the Old and New Testaments, the mother of Jesus and the beloved disciple at the foot of the Cross and concluded.

So, what have we discovered about the mother of Jesus? We have discovered that the mother of Jesus is deeply and intimately connected to Jesus as a mother. This is why the narrator used the honorary title mother to refer to her instead of using her name. Her title clarifies her relationship with Jesus. It indicates her closeness and intimate relationship with her son, Jesus. She is the mother of Jesus and of the Church, a new family of God created at the scene of the cross by Jesus himself. The mother of Jesus plays the role of a textual signal because she marks the beginning and the end of the public ministry of Jesus. She also represents the collective faith of Israel. Like other women at the foot of the cross, the mother of Jesus accompanied Jesus at his lowest moment of death. She is a great listener since she did not talk while Jesus talked with her. She obeyed the words of her son Jesus at the foot of the cross. She simply followed the words of Jesus. Just as she had instructed the servants in John 2, 5 to follow whatever Jesus would tell them, she now puts into practice the words of Jesus and remains exemplary in following the words of Jesus in practical life. She believed in the words of her son once again. She stands out as a model of faith in Jesus. Her docility to Jesus and following his new proposal to be the mother of the beloved disciple is an exemplary role she is playing in this pericope. One can say that Jesus's mother is faithful, a good companion even in suffering, a good listener, a collaborator as she is with other women, and the beloved disciple at the foot of the cross of Jesus.

CHAPTER III

Theological Implications:
The Role of the Mother of Jesus
(John 2, 1-12; 19, 25-27)

3.0 Introduction

This third chapter is our last chapter. In it we will discuss the theological implications of the exegetical study of the role of the mother of Jesus in John 2, 1-12; 19, 25-27. Its main focus will be on the role of the mother of Jesus in John 2, 1-12; 19, 25-27. It shall accomplish this task by looking at the mother of Jesus as a mother who believed in her son, a problem solver and friend, initiator, organizer, and collaborator. Also, as the commander and a good instructor (John 2,5), a silent listener, a companion of Jesus in good and bad times, and a mother of the beloved disciple and the brethren. As a way of giving in more of my personal contribution. I will discuss what I learned as a reader from this exegetical study of John 2,1-12;19, 25-27 and then conclude this chapter.

3.1 The Role of the Mother of Jesus in John 2, 1-12; 19, 25-27

The mother of Jesus is a title accorded to this very important woman in the gospel of John. Her first role is 'mother of Jesus' in the gospel of John. The text uses the genitives: ἡ μήτηρ τοῦ Ἰησοῦ "the mother of Jesus"

(John 2, 1); ἡ μήτηρ αὐτοῦ, "his mother"[223]; referring to the sister of the mother of Jesus John calls her ἡ ἀδελφὴ τῆς μητρὸς αὐτοῦ, "the sister of the mother of him" or better still, "the sister of his mother" (John 19, 25); Jesus saw τὴν μητέρα, "(his) mother"(John 19, 25); λέγει τῇ μητρί, "says to (his) mother" (John 19, 26). These genitives may be termed "genitive of possession" or "genitive of relationship."[224] Both play a role in clarifying and explaining the relationship between Jesus (son) and his mother, who is not named here. According to the text, she plays the role of a mother in the first place. She stands out as an exemplary mother to learn from. Below are some roles she played in John 2, 1-12; 19, 25-27.

3.1.1 She is a mother who believes in her son

The mother of Jesus stands out as the model of faith in her son. She is a mother who is faithful to her motherly role and her son. She expressed faith in her son. Immediately, she noticed a challenge of lack of wine at the wedding feast, so she set out to look for the solution to the problem. Instead, she demonstrated great faith that her son Jesus could do something to change the situation for the better. For this reason, she went and expressed to him confidently, saying, οἶνον οὐκ ἔχουσιν, "They have not wine" (John 2, 3). This is why, when her son responded to her saying, τί ἐμοὶ καὶ σοί, γύναι; οὔπω ἥκει ἡ ὥρα μου, "what to me and to you woman, my hour is not yet come"(John 2, 4). She did not get discouraged or even waste time discussing or arguing with him. She went straight to the servants

---

[223] In a literal translation it would be "the mother of him" but I prefer using "his mother" to have a better nuance in English language.

[224] According to Bechard, genitive of possession defines the *nomen regens* through naming the owner or the one who possesses it. He also explains that the "genitive of relationship" is that type of genitive which denotes "a relationship" defining the "*nomen regens* by naming its source/origin" through "naming the person/class to which it belongs". Thus, between Jesus and his mother there is a relationship of belonging to each other as son and mother. See D. P. Béchard., *Syntax of the New Testament Greek*. A Student's Manual (Rome 2018) 18-19.

and commanded them to do what Jesus would ask them to do (John 2, 5). This was a demonstration of great faith or belief in her son and in what he was able to do. She seemed convinced that Jesus would do something to solve the problem. Jesus was moved, and he performed the sign in John. He performed the sign of changing water to wine and, indeed, a better wine (John 2, 10). Her faith seems to have connected her heart with the heart of Jesus. In a sense, they seemed to have some telepathy, a deep connection. This is also a form of confidentiality and belief in the talents and gifts that her son carried in his life. Mothers of today can learn from this to trust, believe, and have faith in their children as they interact with them.

3.1.2 A Problem solver and friend.

In Cana of Galilee, the mother of Jesus is portrayed as a problem solver. She noticed that there was no wine, and she told her son Jesus οἶνον οὐκ ἔχουσιν, "They have not wine" (John 2, 3). She did not stop there, for she searched for a solution. She initiated and followed the process till the problem was solved. Through her intervention, the problem was solved. The text reveals that a sign occurred since τὸ ὕδωρ οἶνον γεγενημένον, "the water had become wine" (John 2, 9). This shows us that she is a problem solver and, indeed, a friend one could count on.[225] From the lack of wine to the presence of wine and even a better wine. The steward, who never knew where this good wine came from, confirmed that this particular wine was better than the previous one, saying, πᾶς ἄνθρωπος πρῶτον τὸν καλὸν οἶνον τίθησιν καὶ ὅταν μεθυσθῶσιν τὸν ἐλάσσω· σὺ τετήρηκας τὸν καλὸν οἶνον ἕως ἄρτι, "every man first sets out the good wine and when they might have drunk freely the inferior. You have kept the good wine until now" (John 2, 10). The steward confirmed that this later wine provided

---

[225] Don Tonino Bello was probably right to assert that "Maria, un' amica su cui contare" an Italian expression meaning "Maria, a friend you can count on." T. Bello., *Maria. Serva di Dio e del mondo* (Padova 2010)112.

was better in terms of quality than the earlier type. This means that the Mother of Jesus initiated and sustained a transformative action leading to the best solution to the problem of lack of wine. This identifies her as a problem solver. Mothers can imitate her problem-solving attitude in their own families and the different groups they find themselves in. This role is relevant even to all of us. We should not be discouraged in times of problems or lack of something but look for a solution. We should learn to identify the problems in our environment and go forward to find solutions to them. This requires the capacity to discern who has the capacity or strength or required gifts and talents or power to help us solve the problem at hand. As a problem solver, she demonstrated that she is just the agent of the real problem solver, Jesus, her son. She did not start looking for the solution within herself but reached out to her son, the performer of the sign and the one who brought forth the solution. The mother of Jesus possesses a problem-solving attitude and goes forth to initiate the process of solving the problem, but she remains a pointer to the authentic problem solver Jesus. When confronted with situations of lack, we should run to her and, together with her, go to Jesus, who will solve our problems.

3.1.3 She is the initiator, organizer, and Collaborator

She took the initiative[226] by taking the whole situation at hand and took the first step to move towards solving it as she talked it out with her son Jesus (John 2, 3). She organized those whom she thought would help bring forth the transformative action. She did not do it alone but involved Jesus (John 2, 3) and the servants (John 2, 5). Jesus would later ask the servants to take the product of wine to the steward (John 2, 8), hence involving him too. The mother of Jesus took the initiative, organized the

---

[226] This is why Don Tonino Bello refers to her as "Donna del primo passo"(an Italian phrase meaning "First step woman" or better still, a woman who takes initiative), T. Bello., *Maria. Serva di Dio e del mondo,* 83.

people, and allowed for collaboration since everyone played their part in bringing forth the final product, a solution to the problem. She is the one who noticed that there was a problem. The text does not tell us that someone explicitly told her about it. The same text does not reveal that someone explicitly asked her to solve the problem of lack of wine, but she took the initiative. She began the process of addressing or finding the solution at Cana of Galilee. As seen in her request, she informed her son of the situation (John 2, 3). By doing so, she already started organizing this action to take shape and seeking a collaborative effort. She realized that alone, she would not be able to do it. She called on the help of her son and also the servants (John 2, 3. 5). She organized the servants, telling them to do whatever Jesus told them (John 2, 5). This enabled the servants to be prepared to meet Jesus and to follow his instructions. In other words, The mother of Jesus took the initiative to do something to transform the situation, organized different protagonists to be involved in the process to play their roles, and so created a collaborative ministry towards getting a solution to the problem of lack of wine at this wedding feast. Even at the cross of Jesus, she never went there alone; she was in the company of other people. Her collaborative skills are also seen at the foot of the cross when she was with the other three women named in John 19, 25 and the beloved disciple of Jesus (John 19, 26).

3.1.4 The commander and a good instructor (John 2, 5)

She used the imperative verb ποιήσατε, which is meant to give a command. This text reveals that the mother of Jesus commanded the servants, saying ὅ τι ἂν λέγῃ ὑμῖν ποιήσατε, " whatever anyhow he may say to you do" (John 2, 5). The verb ποιήσατε morphologically is aorist, imperative, active, second person, plural of the verb ποιέω.[227] An

---

[227] Cf. M. Zerwick., — M. Grosvenor., *A Grammatical Analysis of the Greek New Testament,* 290.

imperative form is used to give a command. The one who commands are a commander. In this case, the mother of Jesus is the one commanding the servants. She is a commander. She is a commander, for she commanded the servants to do something that later led to the fulfillment of the performance of the first sign by Jesus (John 2, 11). Any mother has to learn from the mother of Jesus to be a commander for the good things to happen in the lives of the families, children, or people they meet daily. The command of the mother of Jesus is also an instruction to the same servants. She instructed them and prepared them psychologically, making them ready and willing to act on whatever Jesus would later ask them to do. It made them do all that Jesus asked them to do without problems. They obeyed his words without questioning or hesitation because the mother of Jesus had already instructed them. This means the mother of Jesus was a good instructor. She instructed them confidently.[228]

3.1.5 A Silent Listener

The Mother of Jesus remained silent and listened to her son at the moment of his suffering at the foot of the cross. She was right there under the cross. She never uttered a word (John 19, 25-27) but listened and silently responded positively to what her son said, "Woman, Behold your Son" (John 19, 26), and she trusted wholeheartedly. She went with the beloved disciple as her very own son.[229]

---

[228] Senior notes that she gave "confident" instruction to the attendants" (John 2, 5). D. Senior., *The Passion of Jesus in the Gospel of John*, 112.

[229] According to Zumstein, the mother of Jesus remained in a total silence and in a passive mood. She and the beloved disciple only realized and fulfilled the instructions that Jesus gave them from the Cross. See J. Zumstein, *The Mother of Jesus and the Beloved Disciple*, 642. It is not surprising when Don Tonino Bello expressed that "Maria è una mamma che ascolta. Sempre. Anche con le lacrime" (an Italian expression meaning that "Mary is a mother who listens always even with tears"), T. Bello., *Maria. Serva di Dio e del mondo*, 116.

3.1.6 A companion of Jesus in good and bad times

She accompanied Jesus in joyful and festive moments of his life and at the moment of his suffering on the cross. She accompanied her son to a feast celebrating a marriage at Cana of Galilee. This is a good moment in the life of her son. Her son Jesus was able to enjoy his life with family members and friends in good times at a marriage ceremony (John 2, 1-12). She did not end there; she also accompanied him even at his low moments of life when he was in pain and suffering at the cross. She did it with her silence and simply being present to accompany him (John 19, 25-27).

3.1.7 A Mother of the beloved disciple and the brethren

When Jesus introduced his mother to the beloved disciple, he presented her to the beloved disciple, saying, "Behold, your mother!" (John 19, 27). In this way, Jesus gave his mother to the beloved disciple with the responsibility of being a mother to him. In the description of the narrative pericope, the mother of Jesus progressed from "his mother" to "the mother" to "woman" and finally to "your mother." The beloved disciple became the son of the mother of Jesus. This is a new relationship of son and mother made up by Jesus himself on the cross. This also means that the beloved disciple became the brother of Jesus.[230] Craig Koester maintained that "the beloved disciple is the first of many brethren."[231] Jesus has created a new family of those related to him by faith, a family

---

[230] J. L. Ressseguie., "The Beloved Disciple: The Ideal point of View", 543.

[231] Koester., *Symbolism*, 243. Resseguie explains that, Before this scene, the term "brother" was used to mean the people who were related to Jesus by way of blood relationship (John 2, 12; 7, 3. 5) but after the event of the resurrection of Jesus, the term "brother" refers to those people who are related to Jesus by way of faith (20, 17). The beloved disciple is therefore the first of the brothers of Jesus who are related to Jesus by faith. This even deepens and reinforces his relationship with Jesus. He is superior to other disciples since he was the only male disciple present at the cross of Jesus. Cf. J. L. Ressseguie., "The Beloved Disciple: The Ideal point of View", 543.

of believers.[232] In this way, the mother of Jesus became the mother of the beloved disciple and those who believe in Jesus. We may conclude that she is the mother of the beloved disciple and the brethren, the church. She is the symbol of the believers in Jesus, her son.[233] The beloved disciple treated her as his own mother. His symbolic treatment of the mother of Jesus is an opening for further Marian symbolizing in the church.[234]

3.2 What I learned as a reader from the exegetical study of John 2, 1-12;19, 25-27

These texts may lead a reader to learn so much from the role of the mother of Jesus. Personally, I learned from her the following. That in life, I have to be faithful to the words of Jesus as his mother instructed and demonstrated in her personal conviction and belief in him (2, 5). Just as she took the initiative, I can do the same. I also learned from her to be an organizer and collaborator and to always ask Jesus and leave him space to decide while I continue preparing myself and working on and believing that he will certainly do something to respond to my plea. She taught me with her willingness to accompany her son in good and bad times. It is a challenge always to accompany the people I know and love in good and bad times.

---

[232] Lindars, *John*, 578-580. This is what Resseguie calls "the first of a new spiritual family (19, 26 -27)," J. L. Ressseguie., "The Beloved Disciple: The Ideal point of View", 549.

[233] See D. Senior., *The Passion of Jesus in the Gospel of John*, 114, where he pointed out that "the mother of Jesus—"the woman" is symbolic of those who seek salvation and of that people who have longed for and will in fact give birth to the messiah, Jesus. That 'birthing' takes place at the cross when Jesus completes his work and returns to the Father. The first impact of Jesus' death-anticipated in 19:25-27-is the birth of the Johannine community...giving birth to the Church is, in John's theology, the first consequence and the first sign of Jesus' redemptive death. The entrusting of the mother of Jesus to the Beloved Disciple is an exquisite symbol of that..."

[234] Cf. R. E. Brown., et al (eds)., *Mary in the New Testament*, 289.

On his part, the beloved disciple taught me a great deal, too, as he took the mother of Jesus immediately after he had listened to the words of Jesus(John 19, 27b). This leaves me with a question, "if I were in his position, would I have reacted immediately as he did? I feel invited by his action to always invite the mother of Jesus into my personal life and ministry and even allow her to be in my own home, life, and actions. To allow her to accompany me in my personal and communal life in the church and, above all, in my priestly ministry and vocation as a Vincentian missionary priest dedicated to the service and evangelization of the poor in the spirit of St. Vincent de Paul under the motherly protection and accompaniment of our lady of the miraculous medal.

The servants (John 2, 7-8) taught me with their readiness, no questioning the mother of Jesus as to why she was telling them to follow what Jesus would tell them to do. Their willingness and, to a certain extent, believing the words of the mother of Jesus and going ahead to follow what Jesus told them is something that has especially touched me too. Jesus knew how to distinguish times for everything. He was concerned about the hour in John 2, 4, which had not yet arrived. He knew to see the difference between times of events. He was aware that he was just at the beginning of his ministry. Later, the hour arrived for him to hand over his mother to the beloved disciple (John 19, 26). So, each event had its own timing for him. Even though he made exceptions at Cana and did what his mother requested, he knew the hour had not yet come. Thus, what he did was a sign through which he manifested his glory (John 2, 11). I learned that in life, I need to discern the different moments to do different things well. Jesus remains an example in this discernment process.

What have you learned as you read the book?

3.3 Conclusion

In this third chapter, the emphasis was on the theological implications of the exegetical study of John 2, 1-12;19, 25-27. We looked at the role of the mother of Jesus as an exemplary mother. We have discovered that the mother of Jesus is a woman of faith. Her role in John 2, 1-12; 19, 25-27 stands out as a mother who believed in her son, a problem solver and friend, initiator, organizer, and collaborator, the commander and a good instructor (John 2,5), a silent listener, a companion of Jesus in good and bad times, and a mother of the beloved disciple and the brethren. As a reader, I learnt to try and be faithful to the words of Jesus as she commanded, take initiative in times when people around me suffer or have some kind of challenge that I can do something about. She challenges the reader to embrace the spirit of accompaniment. To accompany the people, we know in both good and bad times as she did with her son. The reader could embrace the opportunity by inviting the mother of Jesus accompany him or her in both good and bad times as she did with Jesus. This could happen even to the extent of inviting her into our homes as the beloved disciple did.

As a reader and a Vincentian missionary priest, I feel invited by this study to allow her to accompany me in my personal and communal life in the church and in my priestly ministry and vocation as a Vincentian missionary priest dedicated to the service and evangelization of the poor in the spirit of St. Vincent de Paul under the motherly protection and accompaniment of our lady of the miraculous medal.

Also, as a reader, the servants (John 2, 7-8) taught me with their readiness, no questioning the mother of Jesus as to why she was telling them to follow what Jesus would tell them to do. Their willingness and, to a certain extent, believing the words of the mother of Jesus and going ahead to follow what Jesus told them is something that has especially touched me. Jesus knew how to distinguish times for everything. He was concerned about the hour in John 2, 4, which had not yet arrived. He knew how to see the difference between times of events. He was aware that he was just at the beginning of his ministry. Later, the hour arrived for him to hand over his mother to the beloved disciple (John 19, 26). So, each event had its own timing for him. Even though he made exceptions at Cana and did what his mother requested, he knew the hour had not yet come. Thus, what he did was a sign through which he manifested his glory (John 2, 11). As a reader, I learned that in life, I need to discern the different moments to do different things well. Jesus remains an example in this discernment process.

GENERAL CONCLUSION

The first chapter of this book has done an exegetical study of John 2,1-12 with a focus on the mother of Jesus at the wedding of Cana of Galilee (John 2, 1-12). Here, John begins his presentation of the public ministry of Jesus with a narrative of the pericope concerned with the first sign of Jesus. This episode reveals the glory of Jesus and the role of the mother of Jesus as an intercessor and model of trusting faith in Jesus. It further reveals to us that the mother of Jesus is a commander (John 2, 5), an organizer, a problem solver, initiative taker, a good and conscious companion to Jesus in times of celebrations. She is a woman who never takes offense.[235] This text led the disciples to believe in Jesus (John 2, 11). It also invites the reader to believe in Jesus. This pericope also highlights the last words of the mother of Jesus and the importance of obedience to the word of Jesus.

This chapter has exegetically studied and presented preliminary matters: context of John 2, 1-12 (the immediate context of John 2, 1-12; the global context of John 2, 1-12), delimitation of John 2, 1-12, textual criticism of John 2, 1-12, text and translation of John 2,1-12, narrative structure of John 2,1-12 according to Matand, brief explanation of

---

[235] For example, in John 2,4 Jesus called his mother "woman" and she never bothered about it.

the concentric structure of Matand, narrative analysis of John 2, 1-12 : initial situation presented in John 2, 1-2 (Καὶ τῇ ᾑμέρᾳ τῇ τρίτη , "and on the third day" in John 2,1; γάμος ἐγένετο, "a wedding took place" in John 2,1; ἐν Κανὰ τῆς Γαλιλαίας, "in Cana of Galilee" in John 2,1), main characters were introduced in John 2, 1-2 as being ἡ μήτηρ τοῦ Ἰησοῦ, "the mother of Jesus" (2,1) and οἱ μαθηταὶ αὐτοῦ, "his disciples" (John 2, 2). It discussed also: the action of the mother of Jesus in an attempt to solve the problem in John 2, 3-5 : οἶνον οὐκ ἔχουσιν, "they have not wine" (John 2, 3); τί ἐμοὶ καὶ σοί, γύναι; "what to me and to you, woman?" (John 2, 4); ἡ ὥρα , "the hour" (John 2, 4); ὅ τι ἂν λέγῃ ὑμῖν ποιήσατε, "do whatever he tells you" (John 2, 5); the mother of Jesus turned τοῖς διακόνοις "to the servants"(John 2, 5) and the importance of the instruction of the mother of Jesus in John 2, 5. It also handled the transformative action (John 2, 6-8), the reaction of the steward (John 2, 9-10), and final situation (John 2, 11-12). It continued and discussed the key elements in John 2, 1-12 by looking at the term "Sign" in John 2, 11 (the purpose of the sign: revelation of his glory as in John 2, 11; the usefulness of the glory of Jesus revealed in John 2, 11), setting of John 2,1-12 by considering the place to be Cana of Galilee as presented in John 2, 1; the third day as in John 2, 1; and the wedding custom in John 2, 2-3a. We also studied the intratextual and intertextual links that this pericope has with other texts of both the Old and New Testaments. Last but not least, in this chapter we looked at the mother of Jesus at the wedding at Cana of Galilee (John 2, 1-12) and concluded.

It is worth noting that in John 2, 1-12, the narrator has presented to us the first sign performed by Jesus at a wedding feast of Cana of Galilee. His deeds are generally called "signs" in the gospel of John. These signs are not the end in themselves but indicators of the work of God in the world. Thompson maintains that these signs reveal the identity of Jesus "as the messiah and son of God".[236] This narrative text presenting the "first" of the series of signs that Jesus performed serves to inaugurate the public ministry of Jesus in the gospel of John. This first sign shows divine presence and intervention in human suffering and complex situations. It reveals the glory and the identity of Jesus. This pericope also has revealed to us that the mother of Jesus, by nature, is caring, practical, observant, shows initiative, is empathetic, and plays a great role in the revelation of Jesus. It was through her request to Jesus that the public, messianic, and Christological ministry of Jesus was inaugurated in John 2, 1-12 by this first sign. She is a catalyst that led to the belief of the disciples in Jesus.[237] This text points to the significance of obedience as the mother of Jesus said to the servants, "Do whatever he tells you" (John 2, 5). This was the last speech that the mother of Jesus made in the gospel of John. This brings the importance of the "spoken word" in the old and new order. By his word, Jesus spoke to the servants, and the sign of water changed into wine was done. This is also true of the second sign at Cana (John 4, 46-54). We remember here the old order which came to exist by the power of the creative word of God in Gen 1, 1-2.3.

The second chapter was dedicated to the exegetical study of John 19, 25-27. The main focus was on the mother of Jesus at the foot of the cross (John 19, 25-27). This chapter was introduced, then we discussed the preliminary matters that included context of John 19, 25-27, delimitation of John 19, 25-27, an issue of exegetical interpretation in John 19, 25 (two women, three women, four women), text and translation of John 19, 25-27, narrative structure and analysis : plot of John 19, 25-27 (initial situation in John 19, 25; complication (John 19, 26a); transformative action (John 19, 26b-27a); and we finally looked at the resolution and

---

[236] Cf. M. M. Thompson., *John. A Commentary* (NTL; Louisville 2015)64. Indeed, the disciples acknowledged the identity of Jesus as messiah (John 1,45.49).

[237] Bennema, *Encountering Jesus*, 75.

final situation in John 19, 27b. We also discussed key elements in John 19, 25-27 as being the women by the cross (John 19, 25); γύναι, "woman" (John 19, 26a); and ἀπ' ἐκείνης τῆς ὥρας "from that hour" (John 19, 27). Furthermore, in this chapter we considered setting of John 19, 25 – 27, intratextual and Intertextual connections with other texts within the Old and New Testaments, the mother of Jesus and the beloved disciple at the foot of the Cross and the chapter was concluded.

In this second chapter we discovered that the mother of Jesus is deeply and intimately related to Jesus as a mother. This is why the narrator used the honorary title mother to refer to her instead of using her name. Her title clarifies her relationship with Jesus. Her titles indicate her closeness and intimate relationship with her son, Jesus. She is the mother of Jesus and of the Church, a new family of God created at the scene of the cross by Jesus himself. The mother of Jesus plays the role of a textual signal because she marks the beginning and the end of the public ministry of Jesus. She also represents the collective faith of Israel. Like other women at the foot of the cross, the mother of Jesus accompanied Jesus at his lowest moment of death. She is a great listener since she did not talk while Jesus talked with her. She obeyed the words of her son Jesus at the foot of the cross. She simply followed the words of Jesus. Just as she had instructed the servants in John 2, 5 to follow whatever Jesus would tell them, she now puts into practice the words of Jesus and remains exemplary in following the words of Jesus in practical life. She believed in the words of her son. She stands out as a model of faith in Jesus. Her docility to Jesus and following his new proposal to be the mother of the beloved disciple is an exemplary role she is playing in this text. One can say that Jesus's mother is faithful, a good companion, good listener, and a collaborator.

In our third chapter we have studied the theological implications of the exegetical study of John 2, 1-12; 19, 25-27 with a thematic focus on the role of the mother of Jesus. In John 2, 1-12; 19, 25-27 her role stands out as a mother who believed in her son, a problem solver and friend, initiator, organizer, collaborator, commander and a good instructor (John 2,5), a silent listener, a companion of Jesus in good and bad times, and a mother of the beloved disciple and the brethren. As a reader, I learnt from her to be faithful to the words of Jesus as she commanded, take initiative in times when people around me suffer and in need of help. She challenges the reader to embrace the spirit of accompaniment. To accompany the people, we know in both good and bad times as she did with her son. The reader could embrace the opportunity by inviting the mother of Jesus to accompany him or her in both good and bad times as she did with Jesus. This could happen even to the extent of inviting her into our private personal homes as the beloved disciple did.

Generally speaking, one would consider the role of the mother of Jesus in John as being a role model of faith and discipleship as she demonstrated it with relentless trust in her son Jesus (John 2, 3b -5). She is a mediator, intercessor, a prototype of a Christian, representative of Judaism or Jewish Christianity or, better still, of the church. She is a good companion of Jesus in good times (feast of Cana of Galilee) and bad times (at his dying moment at the cross). The mother of Jesus stands out as the representative of the Church and discipleship. She is the mother of the family that Jesus created at the foot of the cross. She is a textual signal who marks the beginning and the end of the public ministry of Jesus. The mother of Jesus is a co-redemptrix with her dying son Jesus. She is the mother of Christ and human beings. Her maternal role is generated by means of faith. Thus, she is both a spiritual and universal mother at the foot of the cross. Indeed, she is a divine mother. She is a good instructor as she instructed the servants well, and they followed the words of Jesus as she had instructed them.

Therefore, she is a major contributor towards the transformative action of Jesus because her request provoked the inauguration of the public, messianic, and Christological ministry of Jesus to be done in the first sign (John 2,1-12). She is a catalyst who led to the belief of the disciples in Jesus. She invited the servants to obey the words of Jesus (John 2, 5). She is portrayed as an observant, caring, practical, and realistic person. She took initiative, showed empathy, and played a role in the revelation of her son Jesus. She is related to Jesus as his mother, and this is revealed in the usage of the genitive of relationship explained already in chapter three. She is a commander, silent listener, problem solver and friend, initiator, organizer and collaborator, a good companion at all times, and a mother of the beloved disciple and the brethren.

The name of the mother of Jesus is not mentioned in the gospel of John since few Christians would be unaware of the name of Jesus' mother since Mark, Matthew, and Luke were in circulation. Even though John was independent, he was probably aware of the information circulated in the early church. This title 'the mother of Jesus' referred to an honorary title given to her and was used to emphasize her role, which she fulfills in the Gospel.

BIBLIOGRAPHY

ABRAMS, M. H., *A Glossary of Literary Terms* (Fort Worth [7]1999).

ALLEGRA, G. M., *Il Cuore Immacolato di Maria* (Acireale 1991).

BAROSSE, T., "The Seven Days of the New Creation in St. John's Gospel", *CBQ* 21 (1959) 507-516.

BARRET, C. K., *The Gospel according to John*. An Introduction with Commentary and Notes on the Greek Text (Philadelphia 1978).

_____ , *The Gospel of John and Judaism*. Translated from the German (trans. SMITH, D. M.) (Philadelphia, 1975).

BAUCKHAM, R., *The Testimony of the Beloved Disciple*. Narrative, History, and Theology in the Gospel of John (Grand Rapids 2007).

_____ , *Gospel Women. Studies of the Named Women in the Gospels* (Grand Rapids 2002).

BEASLEY-MURRAY, G. R., *John* (WBC 36; Waco, TX 1987).

_____ , *John* (WBC 36; Waco, TX [2]1999).

BÉCHARD, D. P., *Syntax of the New Testament Greek*. A Student's Manual (Rome 2018).

BECK, D. R., *The Discipleship Paradigm*. Readers and Anonymous Characters in the Fourth Gospel (Bis 27; Leiden 1997).

BELLO, T., MARIA. *Serva di Dio e del Mondo* (Padova 2010).

BENNEMA, C., *Encountering Jesus*. Character Studies in the Gospel of John (Colorado 2009).

BLINZLER, J., *Die Brüder und Schwester Jesu* (SBS 21; Stuttgart 1967).

BRANT, J. A., *John* (PCNT; Grand Rapids, MI 2011).

BRAUN, F. M., *Jean le théologien et son évangile dans l'église ancienne*. Études bibliques (Paris 1959).

BRODIE, T. L., *The Gospel according to John*. A Literary and Theological Commentary (New York 1993).

BROWN, R. E., *The Gospel According to John*. 2 Vols. (AB 29, 29A; Garden City, N.Y 1966-1970).

——————, *The Gospel According to John I-XII*. A New Translation with Introduction and Commentary (AYB 29; New Haven — London 2008).

——————, et al (eds)., *Mary in the New Testament*. A Collaborative Assessment by Protestant and Roman Catholic Scholars (New York — Mahwah, 1978).

——————, *The Death of the Messiah* (New York 1994) I.

BRUNNER, F. D., *The Gospel of John*. A Commentary (Grand Rapids 2012).

BRUNS, J. E., *The Art and Thought of John* (New York, 1969).

BURY, R. G., *The Fourth Gospel and the Logos-Doctrine* (Cambridge 1940).

CALVIN, J., *Commentary on the Gospel according to John*. 2 Vols. (trans. WILLIAM, P.) (Edinburgh,1987).

CARSON, D. A., *The Gospel According to John* (Grand Rapids 1991).

CARY, M., — HAARHOFF, T. J., *Life and Thought in the Greek and Roman World* (London ⁴1946).

COLLINS, R. F., "The Representative figures of the Fourth Gospel," *DRev* 94 (1976) 24-46, 118-132.

COLOE, M. L., "The Mother of Jesus: A Woman Possessed", *Character Studies in the Fourth Gospel*. Narrative Approaches to Seventy Figures in John (ed. S. A. HUNT) (Tübingen 2013).

COLWELL, E. C., — TITUS, E. L., *The Gospel of the Spirit*. A Study in the Fourth Gospel (New York 1953).

CONWAY, C. M., *Men and Women in the Fourth Gospel*: Gender and Johannine Characterization. SBLDS 167 (Atlanta, 1999).

CULPEPPER, R. A., *Anatomy of the Fourth Gospel*. A Study in Literary Design (Philadelphia 1983).

DAUER, A., *Die Passionsgeschichte in Johannesevangelium*. Eine traditionsgeschichtliche und theologische Untersuchung zu Joh 18,1-19,30 (SANT 30; München 1972).

DE LA POTTERIE, I., *La Passion de Jésus Selon L'évangile de Jean* (LiBi 73; Paris, 1986).

DERRETT, J. D. M., *Law in the New Testament* (London 1970).

DUNN, J. D. G., *Baptism in the Holy Spirit*. A Re-examining of the New Testament Teaching on the Gift of the Spirit in Relation to Pentecostalism Today (SBT 2/15; (London 1970).

ELLIS, P. F., *The Genius of John*. A Composition-Critical Commentary on the Fourth Gospel (Collegeville, 1984).

FEUILLET, A., *Johannine Studies* (trans. E. C. THOMAS) (Staten Island, N. Y 1964).

——————— , *Maria*. Madre del Messia, Madre della Chiesa (Milano 2004).

FLUSSER, D., *Judaism and the Origins of Christianity* (Jerusalem,1988).

FREY, J., *Die Johanneische Eschatologie II*. Das johanneische Zeitverständnis (WUNT 110; Tübingen, 1998).

GLASSON, T. F., *Moses in the Fourth Gospel* (SBT 40; Naperville 1963).

HAENCHEN, E., *A Commentary on the Gospel of John*. 2 Vols. (eds. R. W. FUNK. — U. BUSSE) (Philadelphia 1984).

HAMBLY, W.F., "Creation and Gospel: A Brief Comparison of Genesis 1,1-2,4 and John 1,1-2,12", *SE* 5 (1968) 69-74.

HANHART, K., "The Structure of John i 35-iv 54", *Studies in John Presented to Professor Dr. J. N Sevenster on the Occasion of His Seventieth Birthday* (ed. W. C. VAN UNNIK) (NovTSup 24; Leiden 1970) 22-46.

HARTENSTEIN, J., *Charakterisierung im Dialog*. Maria Magdalena, Petrus, Thomas und die Mutter Jesu im Johannesevangelium im Kontext anderer frühchristlicher Darstellungen (NTOA/SUNT 64; Göttingen, 2007).

HOSKYNS, E. C., "Genesis I-III and St. John's Gospel", *JTS* 21/83 (April 1919) 210-218.

JEREMIAS, J., *The Parables of Jesus* (New York ²1972).

JUDGE, E.A., *Rank and Status in the World of the Caesars and St. Paul*. Broadhead Memorial Lecture 1981 (Christchurch, N. Z 1982).

KEENER, C. S., *Paul, Women and Wives*. Marriage and Women's Ministry in the Letters of Paul (Peabody 1992).

——————— , "Marriage", *DNTB* (eds. C. A. Evans — S. Porter) (Downers Grove 2000).

——————, *Revelation*. NIV Application Commentary (Grand Rapids 2000).

——————, *A Commentary on the Gospel of Matthew* (Grand Rapids 1999).

——————, *Gospel of John*. A Commentary (Grand Rapids 2003) I.

——————, *Gospel of John*. A Commentary (Grand Rapids 2010) II.

KIRBY, J. C., *Ephesians*. Baptism and Pentecost: An Inquiry into the Structure and Purpose of the Epistle to the Ephesians (Montreal 1968).

KOESTER, C., *Symbolism in the Fourth Gospel*. Meaning, Mystery, Community (Minneapolis ²2003).

KURZ, W. S., "The Beloved Disciple and Implied Readers," *BTB* 19 (1989) 100-107.

LIEU, J.M., "The Mother of the Son in the Fourth Gospel," *JBL* 117/1 (1998) 61-77.

LINCOLN, A. T., "The Beloved Disciple as Eyewitness and the Fourth Gospel as Witness," *JSNT* 85 (2002) 3-26.

LINDARS, B., *John*. New Testament Guides (Sheffield 1990).

MACKOWSKI, R. M., "Scholars' Qanah: A Re-examination of the Evidence in Favor of Khirbet-Qanah", *BZ* 23 (1979) 278 — 284.

MALINA, B. J., — RICHARD, L. R., *Social Science Commentary on the Gospel of John* (Minneapolis 1998).

MALINA, B. J., — NEYREY, J. H., "Honor and Shame in Luke-Acts: Pivotal Values of the Mediterranean World.", *The Social World of Luke-Acts: Models for Interpretation* (ed. J. H. NEYREY) (Peabody 1991) 25-65.

MALINA, B. J., *The New Testament World*. Insights from Cultural Anthropology (Atlanta 1981).

MANELLI, S. M., *Mariologia Biblica* (Frigento 2005).

MARROW, S. B., *The Gospel of John*. A Reading (New York—Mahwah, NJ 1995).

MARTIN, T. W., "Assessing the Johannine Epithet 'the Mother of Jesus'" *CBQ* 60 (1998) 63-73.

MATAND, M. J., "Head-waiter and Bridegroom of the Wedding at Cana: Structure and Meaning of John 2.1-12", *JSNT* 30/1(2007) 55-73.

METZGER, B. M., *A Textual Commentary on the Greek New Testament* (London—New York, 1994).

MICHAELS, J. R., *John* (GNC; San Francisco 1984).

MOLONEY, F. J., "John", *Paulist Biblical Commentary* (eds. Chiu, J. E. A., et al.) (New York—Mahwah, NJ 2018) 1105-1185.

—————————— , *Belief in the Word*. Reading the Fourth Gospel — John 1—4 (Minneapolis 1993).

MULLINS, M., *The Gospel of John*. A Commentary (Dublin 2003).

NOACK, B., "The Day of the Pentecost in Jubilees, Qumran, and Acts", Annual of the Swedish Theological Institute 1 (1962) 73—95.

RESSEGUIE, J. L., *Narrative Criticism of the New Testament*. An introduction (Grand Rapids 2005).

—————————— , "The Beloved Disciple: The Ideal point of View", in Characters Studies in the Fourth Gospel (eds. HUNT, S. A., — TOLMIE, D.F., — ZIMMERMANN, R.) (Tübingen 2013) 537—549.

RICOEUR, P., *De L'interprétation*. Essais sur Freud (L'ordre Philosophique; Paris, 1965).

SCHNACKENBURG, R., *The Gospel According to St. John*. Introduction and Commentary on Chapters 1-4 (trans. K. SMYTH) (New York, 1982) I.

SCHNEIDERS, S. M., "Women in the Fourth Gospel," *The Gospel of John as Literature*. An Anthology of Twentieth-Century Perspectives (M. W. G. STIBBE. ed.,) (NTTS 17; Leiden 1993) 123-143.

SCHÜRMANN, H., "Jesu letzte Weisung. Jo 19,26-27a.", *Ders., Ursprung und Gestalt. Erörterungen und Beinnungen zum Neuen Testament*: Spricht von einem. Rätselwort (1970)13-28.

SCOTT, J. M. C., "John", *Eerdmans Commentary on the Bible* (eds. J. D. G. DUNN — J. W. ROGERSON) (Michigan—Cambridge 2003) 1161-1212.

SEIM, T. K., "Roles of Women in the Gospel of John," *Aspects on the Johannine Literature*. Papers Presented at a Conference of Scandinavian New Testament Exegetes at Uppsala, June 16-19, 1986 (eds. HARTMAN, L., — OLSSON, B.) (Stockholm, 1987) 56-73.

SENIOR, D., *The Passion of Jesus in the Gospel of John* (Collegeville — Minnesota 1991).

SLEEPER, C. F., "Pentecost and Resurrection", *JBL* 84 (1965) 389—399.

STAMBAUGH, J. E., — David, L. B., The *New Testament in Its Social Environment* (LEC 2; Philadelphia, 1986).

STIBBE, M. W. G., *John* (Sheffield 1993).

THE HOLY BIBLE, Revised Standard Version, second catholic Edition (San Francisco 1965).

THYEN, H., *Das Johannes Evangelium* (HNT 6; Tübingen, 2005).

THOMPSON, M. M., *John*. A Commentary (NTL; Louisville 2015).

TOLMIE, D. F., "The Women by the Cross. Creating Contrasts", *Characters Studies in the Fourth Gospel* (eds. Hunt, S. A., — Tolmie, D.F., — Zimmermann, R.) (Tübingen 2013) 618-625.

TOLMIE, D. F., *Narratology and Biblical Narratives*. A Practical Guide (San Francisco, 1999).

VON WAHLDE, U. C., "John", *The Jerome Biblical Commentary for the Twenty-First Century* (eds. J. J. COLLINS., et al) (London— New York ³2022) 1378-1444.

WAETJEN, H. C., The *Gospel of the Beloved Disciple*. A work in Two Editions (New York 2005).

WILLIAMS, R. H., "The Mother of Jesus at Cana. A Social-Science Interpretation of John 2:1-12", *CBQ* 59 (1997) 679-692.

WITHERINGTON, B. III., *Women in the Ministry of Jesus*. A Study of Jesus' Attitudes to Women and Their Roles as Reflected in His Earthly Life (SNTSMS 51; Cambridge 1984).

ZERWICK, M. S. J., — Grosvenor, M., *A Grammatical Analysis of the Greek New Testament* (Rome 2016).

ZUMSTEIN, J., "The Mother of Jesus and the Beloved Disciple: How a New Family is Established under the Cross", *Characters Studies in the Fourth Gospel* (eds. HUNT, S. A., —TOLMIE, D.F., — ZIMMERMANN, R.) (Tübingen, 2013) 641—645.

ABOUT THE AUTHOR

REV. FR. JOHN Bosco Odongo,CM., SSL.

Fr. John Bosco Odongo,CM., born in Uganda on 26th December 1981, is a Roman Catholic Vincentian Missionary Priest, Ordained on 28th May 2016 in Nairobi Kenya. He holds a baccalaureate degree in Philosophy from the Pontifical Urban University in Rome in Italy and a Baccalaureate degree in Sacred Theology from the Pontifical Urban University, Rome in Italy; Diploma in Education Secondary (DES) from Kyambogo University, Kampala in Uganda. He taught Geography and Religious Education at St. Francisca Girls Secondary School, Ibuje Secondary School, and Iceme Girls Secondary School in Uganda. After his priestly Ordination, he taught at the biblical department of Christ the King Major Seminary, Nyeri in Kenya. Subsequently, he served in the formation as the assistant General spiritual director, formator and lecturer at the above-named

Major seminary. He is a biblist holding a Licentiate in Sacred Scriptures (SSL) from the Pontifical Biblical Institute Rome in Italy. Currently, he is pursuing a Doctoral degree in Biblical Theology at Pontifical Gregorian University in Rome, Italy. In an attempt to study and share his faith experience, Fr. John Bosco has founded a number of prayer groups online namely: "Scuola Di Gesu" (Italian for School of Jesus); "Popolo Di Cristo" (People of Christ); "Vita in Cristo international" (Life in Christ International); "Fratelli in Cristo" (brothers and sisters in Christ) and finally the friends of Fr. John Bosco. They are groups that exist mostly on WhatsApp for the sole purpose of sharing the gospel of Jesus Christ and personal faith experiences based on the good news of Jesus Christ. These experiences informed his faith and prayer in a personal walk with Jesus. This book is aimed at encouraging the devotion to the mother of Jesus and with her take up a journey to knowing Jesus better and thereby believe in him and attain eternal life. For questions, clarification, new ideas or consultation contact:johnforchristjesus@gmail.com; Tel: +39 371 382 3802.